THE PROBLEM OF GOD STUDY GUIDE

THE PROBLEM OF

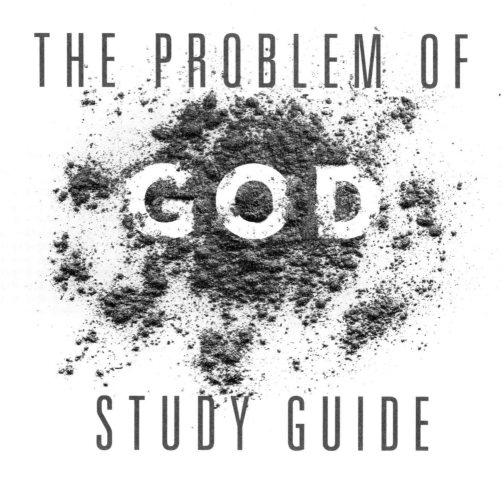

GOD

STUDY GUIDE

ANSWERING A SKEPTIC'S CHALLENGES TO CHRISTIANITY

TEN SESSIONS

MARK CLARK

ZONDERVAN
REFLECTIVE

ZONDERVAN REFLECTIVE

The Problem of God Study Guide
Copyright © 2021 by Mark Clark

Requests for information should be addressed to:
Zondervan, 3900 *Sparks Dr. SE, Grand Rapids, Michigan 49546*

Zondervan titles may be purchased in bulk for educational, business, fundraising, or sales promotional use. For information, please email SpecialMarkets@Zondervan.com.

ISBN 978-0-310-10843-6 (softcover)
ISBN 978-0-310-10844-3 (ebook)

Published in association with the literary agency of The Fedd Agency, Post Office Box 341973, Austin, TX 78734.

Cover design and image: FaceOut Studio
Interior design: Denise Froehlich

Printed in the United States of America

21 22 23 24 25 / LSC / 10 9 8 7 6 5 4 3 2 1

Contents

Introduction vii

How to Use This Guide ix

Session 1: The Problem of Science .1

Session 2: The Problem of God's Existence 17

Session 3: The Problem of the Bible 31

Session 4: The Problem of the Christ Myth. 46

Session 5: The Problem of Evil and Suffering. 62

Session 6: The Problem of Hell 78

Session 7: The Problem of Sex 94

Session 8: The Problem of Hypocrisy 113

Session 9: The Problem of Exclusivity 134

Session 10: The Problem of Jesus 152

Closing Words. 173

Index of Verses Used (by Session) 175

Leading This Group 179

Introduction

Welcome to *The Problem of God Study Guide*. This guide, including ten teaching sessions, is meant to be a companion learning experience to my book, *The Problem of God*. And here's why this study is so important. When my wife, Erin, and I launched Village Church in 2010 from an elementary school gymnasium with fifty people in Vancouver, we wanted our church to be a safe space for skeptics and believers alike. We wanted to be a welcoming place for people who had never stepped foot in a church, and for people who had walked away from it all. I wanted to reach real people who lived in the real world: people who doubted the existence of God, people who thought Christianity was judgmental and narrow-minded, people who spent their free time reading about the latest updates in astrophysics, not the latest Christian bestseller. We wanted to be a church where the Bible was taught and where skeptics and cynics could come to be challenged, ask questions, and maybe even get some answers. Do you know why? Because those people were me. I was a skeptic, a cynic, and a doubter. Even when I became a believer and a pastor, I still lay awake at night with deep philosophical questions that couldn't be answered with the simple suggestion to "just have faith." I had to know the truth, and why the truth existed. That's why this study first came into existence as a sermon series, then as a book, and now as a study guide with teaching sessions. I was certain if I still had some of these questions as a pastor and knew that my skeptical and cynical friends had the same questions, then you probably did, too. And what I discovered was that God has profound answers to the questions we're all asking.

So, if you have the courage to doubt your doubts and to suspend your disbelief, even for a moment, there is a possibility you will actually see something credible on the other side of the veil of your skepticism and cynicism. You will see that the Bible, Jesus, and everything else that orbits around Christianity will hold up under historical, scientific, philosophical, and even literary scrutiny. You will see that Christianity presents a rational and distinct view of origins, meaning, morality, and destiny beyond any other religious or secular worldview. And it's my hope that you see Christianity as the best answer to your questions and your longings—so much so that you're willing to give your life to it.

That's why this study guide and the accompanying video teachings are designed to help you explore the common questions of the human mind: *science, God's existence, the Bible, the Christ Myth, evil and suffering, hell, sex, hypocrisy, exclusivity, and Jesus.* Together we will discover credible answers and evidence in Christianity that actually change people's lives in amazing and tangible ways. While you may have picked this study because it's about God and Christianity, in a sense, it is more about *you*. If you're anything like me, you want evidence to the answers, claims, and ideas before you are willing to accept it. And like you, I don't believe every claim that comes my way simply because someone tells me it's true. I want to wrestle with the questions, the ideas, and the evidence. My hope and prayer is that this study is the safe space you need to wrestle in the place where faith and skepticism meet.

Mark Clark

How to Use
THIS GUIDE

The Problem of God video study is designed to be experienced in a group setting such as a Bible study, Sunday school class, or any small group gathering. Each session begins with a welcome section, two questions to get you thinking about the topic, and a reading from the Bible. You will then watch a video with Mark Clark and engage in some small-group discussion. You will close each session with a time of personal reflection and prayer as a group.

Each person in the group should have his or her own copy of this study guide and a Bible. Multiple translations will be used throughout the study, so whatever translation you have is fine. You are also encouraged to have a copy of *The Problem of God* trade book, as reading the book alongside the curriculum will provide you with deeper insights and make the journey more meaningful. See the "For Next Week" section at the end of each between-studies section for the chapter in the book that corresponds to the material your group is discussing.

To get the most out of your group experience, keep the following points in mind. First, the real growth in this study will happen during your small group time. This is where you will process the content of the teaching for the week, ask questions, and learn from others as you hear what God is doing in their lives. For this reason, it is important for you to be fully committed to the group and attend each session so you can build trust and rapport with the other members. If you choose to only go through the motions, or if you refrain from participating, there is a lesser chance you will find what you're looking for during this study.

Second, remember the goal of your small group is to serve as a place where people can share, learn about God, and build intimacy and friendship. For this reason, seek to make your group a safe place. This means being honest about your thoughts and feelings and listening carefully to everyone else's opinion. (If you are a group leader, there are additional instructions and resources in the back of the book for leading a productive discussion group.)

Third, resist the temptation to fix a problem someone might be having or to correct his or her theology, as that's not the purpose of your small-group time. Also, keep everything your group shares confidential. This will foster a rewarding sense of community in your group and create a place where people can heal, be challenged, and grow spiritually.

Following your group time, reflect on the material you've covered by engaging in the between-session activities. For each session, you may wish to complete the personal study all in one sitting or spread it out over a few days (for example, working on it a half hour a day on different days that week). Note that if you are unable to finish (or even start!) your between-sessions personal study, you should still attend the group study video session. You are still wanted and welcome to the group even if you don't have your "homework" done.

Keep in mind that the videos, discussion questions, and activities are simply meant to kickstart your thoughts so you are both open to what God wants you to hear and also how to apply it to your life. As you go through this study, be open and listen to what God is saying to you as you discover an insightful, fresh perspective of *The Problem of God*.

> **Note:** If you are a group leader, there are additional resources provided in the back of this guide to help you lead your group members through the study.

The Problem of
SCIENCE

In the beginning God created the heavens and the earth.

—GENESIS 1:1

Welcome

I grew up in an exclusively non-Christian social world, where if you believed something with conviction, you would have to test it, so you were able to defend it when challenged. This eventually produced an informed faith rather than an assumed faith in my life, but I had to go through years of struggle to get there. I first heard about Christianity at summer camp when I was nine years old, and I was fascinated by the concept of God. My fascination wasn't strong enough to make me start doing religious things like going to church and reading my Bible, but it did make me sign up for summer camp every year. I would go to camp, sing songs and talk about God with my new friends, and then return home to a very different life.

By the time I hit my early teens, I partied, got high, and stole money so I could continue to get high. It was a cycle I enjoyed until I bumped up against God again at the end of high school. Because of my non-Christian social world, and the conflicting views of God in my family, the summer camp faith of my adolescence quickly translated into the teenage life of a doubter and a skeptic where I was keenly aware of the faith vs. science debate. The argument usually started with the idea that modern science was based on the most current evidence and logical reasoning, while faith was not. And I agreed. I fell for the skeptic's conclusion that the Christian faith was based on ancient evidence and irrational thinking until I started exploring the common myths about the intersection of faith and science. Whether or not to believe existing evidence and theories debated by scientists and theologians alike is based on what we believe about our faith in God.

Share

If you or any of your group members are just getting to know one another, take a few minutes to introduce yourselves. Then, to kick things off, briefly discuss one of the following:

- Share one hope or expectation you have for this study.

    —or—

- What is the most common argument you hear in the debate regarding faith vs. science?

Read

Invite someone to read aloud the following passage as preparation for Mark's teaching. Listen for fresh insights as you hear the verses being read, and then briefly discuss the questions that follow.

PSALM 104

Praise the LORD, my soul.

LORD my God, you are very great;
    you are clothed with splendor and majesty.

The LORD wraps himself in light as with a garment;
    he stretches out the heavens like a tent
    and lays the beams of his upper chambers on their waters.
He makes the clouds his chariot
    and rides on the wings of the wind.
He makes winds his messengers,
    flames of fire his servants.

He set the earth on its foundations;
　　it can never be moved.
You covered it with the watery depths as with a garment;
　　the waters stood above the mountains.
But at your rebuke the waters fled,
　　at the sound of your thunder they took to flight;
they flowed over the mountains,
　　they went down into the valleys,
　　to the place you assigned for them.
You set a boundary they cannot cross;
　　never again will they cover the earth.

He makes springs pour water into the ravines;
　　it flows between the mountains.
They give water to all the beasts of the field;
　　the wild donkeys quench their thirst.
The birds of the sky nest by the waters;
　　they sing among the branches.
He waters the mountains from his upper chambers;
　　the land is satisfied by the fruit of his work.
He makes grass grow for the cattle,
　　and plants for people to cultivate—
　　bringing forth food from the earth:
wine that gladdens human hearts,
　　oil to make their faces shine,
　　and bread that sustains their hearts.
The trees of the LORD are well watered,
　　the cedars of Lebanon that he planted.
There the birds make their nests;
　　the stork has its home in the junipers.
The high mountains belong to the wild goats;
　　the crags are a refuge for the hyrax.

He made the moon to mark the seasons,
    and the sun knows when to go down.
You bring darkness, it becomes night,
    and all the beasts of the forest prowl.
The lions roar for their prey
    and seek their food from God.
The sun rises, and they steal away;
    they return and lie down in their dens.
Then people go out to their work,
    to their labor until evening.

How many are your works, LORD!
    In wisdom you made them all;
    the earth is full of your creatures.
There is the sea, vast and spacious,
    teeming with creatures beyond number—
    living things both large and small.
There the ships go to and fro,
    and Leviathan, which you formed to frolic there.

All creatures look to you
    to give them their food at the proper time.
When you give it to them,
    they gather it up;
when you open your hand,
    they are satisfied with good things.
When you hide your face,
    they are terrified;
when you take away their breath,
    they die and return to the dust.
When you send your Spirit,
    they are created,
    and you renew the face of the ground.

May the glory of the LORD endure forever;
     may the LORD rejoice in his works—
he who looks at the earth, and it trembles,
     who touches the mountains, and they smoke.

I will sing to the LORD all my life;
     I will sing praise to my God as long as I live.
May my meditation be pleasing to him,
     as I rejoice in the LORD.
But may sinners vanish from the earth
     and the wicked be no more.

Praise the LORD, my soul.

Praise the LORD.

What do you notice in this poetic version of the Creation story?

_____

_____

_____

Consider as you listen to Mark's teaching, *what would change about your perspective of the Bible if you understood it from a secularist—or without God—point of view?*

_____

_____

_____

Watch ▶

Play the video segment for session 1. As you watch, use the following outline to record any thoughts or concepts that stand out to you.

NOTES

———— Faith vs. Science ————

The False Dichotomy: Science moves us forward with objective evidence, while faith is ancient and based on irrational conclusions.

———— The Myth of Culture ————

Secularism (Naturalism): A worldview that seeks to eliminate God from society as a whole.

> Faith is like a mental illness, a great cop-out, the excuse to evade the need to think and evaluate evidence.
>
> —RICHARD DAWKINS

> We have names for people who have many beliefs for which there is no rational justification. When their beliefs are extremely common, we call them "religious"; otherwise, they are likely to be called "mad," "delusional," or "psychotic."
>
> —SAM HARRIS

Key Question: But what if faith and reason are not opposed to each other?

———— The Myth of the Church vs. Science ————

> It's actually more rational to believe in God than not.
>
> —MARK CLARK

Philosophy departments now include *theists*, people who believe in God.

> I am convinced that the case for belief in God is inductively so much stronger than the case for unbelief, that true philosophical atheism must be regarded as a superstition.
>
> —DAVID BENTLEY HART

There was no warfare between science and the church. The reality is the church did not persecute Copernicus, or Bruno, or Galileo for scientific theories.

—DAVID LINDBERG

The idea that science and religion are in perpetual conflict is no longer taken seriously by any major historian of science. One of the last remaining bastions of atheism survives at the popular level, namely, the myth that an atheistic fact-based science is permanently at war with a faith-based religion.

—ALISTER MCGRATH

Modern science was conceived out of Christianity.

———— The Myth of Secular Society ————

The university is a twelfth-century Christian invention.
Every single person has a faith position.

I have a prior commitment to materialism. It's not that the methods and institutions of science somehow compel us to accept a material explanation of the phenomenal world. On the contrary, we are forced by our *a priori* adherence to material causes. We cannot allow a divine foot in the door.

—RICHARD LEWONTIN

Science is not just facts; it is also philosophy.

You cannot doubt unprovable Christian belief 'A' except from a position of faith in unprovable non-Christian belief 'B.'

—MARK CLARK

Example: *Resurrection*
Example: *Evolution*

Within me, the horrid doubt always arises whether the convictions of a man's mind, which has been developed from the mind of lower animals, is of any value, or at all trustworthy.

—CHARLES DARWIN

Key Question: Why did we, as humans, ever develop moralistic structures that counter the violent realities of nature?

Star Trek: There was a shift in science and spirituality.

> We can't adjudicate the question of God's existence from the world of physics, from the world of science. It's a NOMA principle: non-overlapping magisterial.
>
> —STEPHEN J. GOULD

The NOMA Principle (non-overlapping magisterial): God transcends science. Science actually points to the existence of God.

> Ever since the creation of the world his invisible nature, namely, his eternal power and deity, has been clearly perceived in the things that have been made. So they are without excuse.
>
> —ROMANS 1:20 RSV

Christianity leans into science, rather than running from it.

> We need to run the ramp of reason before taking the leap of faith. And be people who actually inform our faith positions with the evidence of the world that God has given us.
>
> —MARK CLARK

Group Discussion

Take a few minutes with your group members to discuss what you just watched and explore these concepts in Scripture. Then take time to pray together as a group. Use the space at the end of this session to keep track of prayer requests and group updates.

1. What stood out to you from Mark's teaching on the debate of science vs. faith?

_____

_____

_____

2. How have you specifically encountered this cultural debate over the years?

_____

_____

_____

3. **Read Colossians 1:15–17.** How might we interpret these verses in light of the science vs. faith debate? What is the meaning of Paul's explanation of the supremacy of the Son of God?

_____

_____

_____

4. **Read Ecclesiastes 1:1–18.** The author of Ecclesiastes seems to debate the very things we are talking about today. What does he conclude, and why? How do you identify with the author?

_____

_____

_____

5. How does the NOMA principle help you explain your faith in God when compared to scientific reasoning?

_____

_____

_____

6. What other questions or concerns do you have about the intersection of faith and science?

_____

_____

_____

Pray

Pray as a group before you close your time together. Ask God to open your hearts and minds and allow you to see how God transcends science, and how scientific reasoning and faith actually go hand in hand with one another. Ask God for wisdom in understanding and perspective in your reasoning. Thank God that he reigns in love over the visible and invisible of this world. Use this space to keep track of prayer requests and group updates.

SESSION 1

Between-Sessions
PERSONAL STUDY

Weekly Reflection

Before you begin the between-sessions exercises, briefly review your video notes for session 1. In the space below, write down the *most significant point* you took away from this session.

_____

_____

_____

_____

Take some time to reflect on the material you covered during your group time by engaging in any or all of the following between-sessions exercises. As you read and experience the material, you may want to make a few notes in your guide. The primary goal of these activities is for your own spiritual growth and personal reflection, and they are not a requirement for group participation. If you haven't done so already, read chapter one in *The Problem of God*.

Day 1: The Search for Truth
Read: *John 1:14 and 8:31–47; 1 Thessalonians 5:19–22*

Consider: One of the most powerful and pervasive structures of thought the world has ever known is called secularism. Secularism teaches that because there is no God and no spiritual reality in the universe beyond what we can test, belief in such ideas should be marginalized from public life and discourse. Secularists believe that religious beliefs have been categorically proven false by modern developments in science and technology. And subsequently, secularists believe our religious beliefs must be dismissed. Such is the case in the great debate on science vs. faith.

From a secularist point of view, this debate is an *either/or* perspective. It's a perspective that tells us we can believe in *either* science *or* faith because the two disciplines are mutually exclusive.

But this is a misguided search for truth. It's the overflow of a modern culture that thinks only in sound bites and extremes. The real search for truth requires investigation and a centered approach that takes into consideration *both/and*. In this case, we believe *both* faith *and* science work together to inform our Christian beliefs. But here's the deal: We can believe in a *both/and* approach to science and faith, and yet still subscribe to an *either/or* perspective in other areas of life. Or vice versa. We have an *either/or* perspective of faith and science but welcome a *both/and* approach to the rest of life. Consider your mindset toward the search for truth and life in general.

Reflect: Take a few moments to reflect on your answers to these questions.

In general, do you tend to approach life with an either/or OR both/and perspective when it comes to the truth?

Here are a few examples:

> Your best friend is either your friend or she is a liar. OR she is your best friend and at times tells a lie.
> Your spouse is either in love with you or he's not. OR your spouse is in love with you and some days acts like he doesn't like you.
> Your professor is either an expert or a fake. OR your professor is an expert and sometimes mixes up the details of a topic.
> Your pastor is either a theologian with the correct answers or not. OR your pastor is a theologian with answers and a human who still has questions and doubts.

Now give some examples from your own life:

_____

_____

_____

What is your perspective on the truth of faith and science—is it a both/and OR either/or approach, and why?

_____

_____

_____

According to these passages, what is truth, and why does truth matter?

_____

_____

_____

Pray: Close out your time today by praying to God about your search for truth. May God illuminate the truth for you as you press into him.

Day 2: The Garden of Christianity
Read: *Genesis 1; Psalm 8 and 104; Acts 14:16–18*

Consider: Christian theology is the garden out of which modern science grew because it presented a world with distinct form, complexity, and design. No other worldview, philosophy, or religion of the ancient world offered the unique perspective Christianity did in the fundamental variables that laid the groundwork for scientific inquiry. Here are ten such variables cited by Kenneth Richard Samples:

- *The physical universe is a distinct, objective reality.*
- *The laws of nature exhibit order, patterns, and regularity.*
- *The laws of nature are uniform throughout the physical universe.*
- *The physical universe is intelligible.*
- *The world is good, valuable, and worthy of careful study.*
- *Because the world is not divine and therefore not a proper object of worship, it can be an object of rational study.*
- *Human beings possess the ability to discover the world's intelligibility.*
- *The free agency of the Creator makes the empirical method necessary.*
- *God encourages, even propels, science through his imperative to humans to take dominion over nature.*
- *The intellectual virtues essential to carrying out the scientific enterprises are part of God's moral law.*

From these variables, science drew on the biblical mandate to use reason to explore and investigate. Christianity challenges us to experiment with what we see, believing there is order and uniformity to the universe. This is the garden of Christianity.

Reflect: Take a few moments to reflect on your answers to these questions.

In what ways do you experience the order and uniformity of the universe—in both big and small things? (i.e., changing of the seasons, celestial rhythms, etc.)

_____

_____

_____

What is meaningful about acknowledging Christianity as the "garden" for modern science? Is there another metaphor that comes to mind for you?

_____

_____

_____

How do these passages influence your perspective about modern science?

_____

_____

_____

Pray: Close out your time today by praying to God about this idea of Christianity as the garden of modern science. May you find the truth of God in the rhythms and seasons of creation.

Day 3: People of Faith
Read: _John 4:11–21; Romans 1:18–23; 1 John 4:11–21_

Consider: We must admit we all have faith commitments and we have been a people of faith for thousands of years. Take, for instance, the skeptics who doubt that Jesus Christ really rose from the dead. Why do people reject this? Because they already have faith in something else; they already hold a prior belief that when people die there is no coming back from the dead. But a belief in the finality of death and a belief that nothing can defy the laws of nature are both _unprovable_ conclusions. Even our doubts are a set of alternative beliefs. Skeptics are committed to a lifestyle of consistent doubt. But in choosing not to commit to any one belief about spiritual or ultimate things—even when they feel that they are being open-minded—skeptics miss the inherent irony that to *not* commit to a set of beliefs about spiritual matters is itself a choice to commit to a set of beliefs about spiritual matters. Same with secularism, which is a set of alternative doctrines and beliefs to theism—beliefs that have not been proven and substantiated enough to be taught as the *only* or exclusive way to think as a human being. The fact of the matter is we all have a faith position, an interpretation of reality that does not have definitive proof. Everyone believes in something and makes assumptions about reality that can't be proven through science. Even in the world of science, our faith position predetermines what we accept and believe about science, not the other way around. We live this way without even thinking about it or knowing it. This faith position exists for all of us to help frame reality and give life meaning. It helps to answer our deepest questions regarding identity, environment, origins, and purpose.

Reflect: Take a few moments to reflect on your answers to these questions.

How do your prior held beliefs influence your faith in God or your view about science?

_____

_____

_____

What do these passages tell us about faith? What does faith mean to you?

_____

_____

_____

How do you investigate your faith, or how will you investigate your faith as a result of what you've learned in this session?

_____

_____

_____

Pray: Close out your time today by praying to God about your view of faith. May you find meaning in the Christian faith position.

For Next Week: Read chapter two in *The Problem of God* and use the space below to write any insights or questions from your personal study that you want to discuss at the next group meeting.

Journal, Reflections, and Notes

The Problem of
GOD'S EXISTENCE

He has made everything beautiful in its time.
He has also set eternity in the human heart; yet
no one can fathom what God has done from
beginning to end.

—ECCLESIASTES 3:11

Welcome

At some point in my youth, I decided to believe in nothing. I was a classic skeptic, a doubter. I didn't believe in God at all. But I asked a lot of questions. I was just fifteen years old when my dad died of lung cancer at the age of forty-seven. He never told us he was sick, so I never got to say goodbye. Up until that point, my father was a classic deadbeat dad. He couldn't hold down a job, didn't know how to raise my brother and me, and divided his time between drinking and yelling at football games. I remember the lonely feeling I had a few days after he died, standing over his casket in the funeral home as my mind flooded with questions about God. I began to ponder where exactly my father was, and I asked myself what I believed about God, humankind, eternity, morality, and about my father. Where did he go? Somewhere? Nowhere? It wasn't until two years later when I met a guy named Chris that I really started to examine my questions and my doubts, read the Bible, and pray. Chris was a former drug dealer at my school who had become a follower of Jesus and had been totally transformed. I was intrigued by his life, his questions, and his passion for God. It was then that I started asking if the existence of God was really true. At first, I didn't want to believe that everyone was right about God. The whole popular view of God seemed too convenient, and I was skeptical about convenient things. But then I realized that faith required skepticism. Believing one thing meant you had to challenge and exclude other things, and this was true for believing in the existence of God.

Share 💬

If you or any of your group members are just getting to know one another, take a few minutes to introduce yourselves. Then, to kick things off, briefly discuss one of the following:

- Name one or two commonly accepted critiques about the existence of God or the creation of the universe.

  —or—
- Why do you think we are drawn to reading, watching, and listening to sci-fi?

Read 📖

Invite someone to read aloud the following passage as preparation for Mark's teaching. Listen for fresh insights as you hear the verses being read, and then briefly discuss the questions that follow.

PSALM 145

I will exalt you, my God the King;
and I will praise your name for ever and ever.
Every day I will praise you
and extol your name for ever and ever.

Great is the LORD and most worthy of praise;
his greatness no one can fathom.
One generation commends your works to another;
they tell of your mighty acts.
They speak of the glorious splendor of your majesty—
and I will meditate on your wonderful works.
They tell of the power of your awesome works—
and I will proclaim your great deeds.

They celebrate your abundant goodness
    and joyfully sing of your righteousness.

The LORD is gracious and compassionate,
    slow to anger and rich in love.

The LORD is good to all;
    he has compassion on all he has made.
All your works praise you, LORD;
    your faithful people extol you.
They tell of the glory of your kingdom
    and speak of your might,
so that all people may know of your mighty acts
    and the glorious splendor of your kingdom.
Your kingdom is an everlasting kingdom,
    and your dominion endures through all generations.

The LORD is trustworthy in all he promises
    and faithful in all he does.
The LORD upholds all who fall
    and lifts up all who are bowed down.
The eyes of all look to you,
    and you give them their food at the proper time.
You open your hand
    and satisfy the desires of every living thing.

The LORD is righteous in all his ways
    and faithful in all he does.
The LORD is near to all who call on him,
    to all who call on him in truth.
He fulfills the desires of those who fear him;
    he hears their cry and saves them.

> The LORD watches over all who love him,
>   but all the wicked he will destroy.
>
> My mouth will speak in praise of the LORD.
>   Let every creature praise his holy name
>   for ever and ever.

What new insight do you notice in this passage?

_____

_____

_____

Consider as you listen to Mark's teaching, *how do you explain the greatness of God or the mysteries of the universe created by God?*

_____

_____

_____

Watch ▶

Play the video segment for session 2. As you watch, use the following outline to record any thoughts or concepts that stand out to you.

NOTES

——— The Evidence of God's Existence ———

The moral law within and the starry hosts above.
—AN IDEA ABOUT PEOPLE AND THE UNIVERSE BY IMMANUEL KANT

——— People: The Moral Law Argument ———

We all have an unspoken moral law within us.
Key Question: Where did your moral law come from?

The law stitched within us.

> They show that what the law requires is written on their hearts, while their conscience
> also bears witness and their conflicting thoughts accuse or perhaps excuse them.
>
> —ROMANS 2:15 RSV

——— Starry Hosts Above: The Argument of God's Existence ———

Contingency: If something exists, it has to have a cause.

Edwin Hubble (1930s) discovered the universe is ever-expanding.

> The number of stars involved in this galactic dispersal suggested an astoundingly
> vast Universe. Some galaxies were millions of light-years away. Hubble noticed that
> planets and entire galaxies were hurtling away from one another at fantastic speeds.
> Moreover, space itself seemed to be getting bigger. The Universe was not expanding in
> the background of space. Incredibly, space itself was expanding along with the Universe.
> Scientists realized right away that the galaxies were not flying apart because of some
> mysterious force thrusting them away from each other. Rather, they were moving apart
> because they were once flung apart by a primeval explosion.
>
> —DINESH D'SOUZA

> Everything that begins to exist has to have a cause.
>
> —MARK CLARK

Key Question: Why do you exist? What is the cause of your existence?

> "God is spirit, and those who worship him must worship in spirit and truth."
>
> —JOHN 4:24 RSV

The Second Law of Thermodynamics: The energy in the Earth is actually decreasing (which hints at the finite nature of the universe).

The universe as a flashlight.

The rational answer: *Something* caused the universe to come into existence.

Biology: The DNA of Living Organisms

The Language of God (Francis S. Collins)

> If you were walking along a beach and you came upon a piece of wood, you might say, "This chipped off a tree somewhere. That's its origin." But if you stumbled upon a working watch and you picked it up out of the sand, with all of the intricate design and detail, you would say, "Somebody made this; this points to someone."
>
> —WILLIAM PALEY

The Chances: The chances of our universe coming into existence at all is 1 in 10^{138}.

The Context: The number of seconds in the entire history of the universe is 10^{17}. The number of atoms in the universe is 10^{70}.

> Astrophysicists say there are actually 122 variables that would have had to be fine-tuned in precise values to the million-millionth in order for our universe to have ever come into existence.
>
> —MARK CLARK

The 15 "constants" in play.

> Matter would not have been able to coalesce. There would have been no galaxies, no stars, no planets, and no people.
>
> —FRANCIS COLLINS

> A common-sense interpretation of the facts suggests that a superintellect has monkeyed with physics, as well as chemistry and biology and that there are no blind forces worth speaking about in nature.
>
> —FRED HOYLE

Key Question: When did these laws of physics begin to exist?
Science points to the evidence of God.

If the rate of expansion, one second after the Big Bang, had been smaller by even one part in one-hundred-thousand-million-millionths, the universe would have re-collapsed before it ever reached its present size into a hot fireball. The odds against a universe like ours emerging out of something like the Big Bang are enormous. I think there are religious implications.

—STEPHEN HAWKING

When faced with these kinds of statistics, it takes more faith to believe that our universe came into existence out of nothing rather than the belief that someone created it.

[This] would be like if you were arrested and sentenced to death by a firing squad. And you're positioned against a wall. And there are a hundred trained marksmen shooting at you from twenty feet away. And they all shoot and when the dust clears, you're still standing there, untouched by any bullets, over and over and over and over and over and over and over again for hundreds of years, thousands of years, and you never get hit by a bullet. At what point will someone go, "Wait a minute: someone's monkeying with this. Someone has engineered this"? And how readily would you accept an explanation of chance?

—WILLIAM LANE CRAIG

This defies logic.

Key Question: But what if I don't want to believe in this?

The Multiverse Theory: The reason we can believe in the universe without God's existence is that there are an infinite number of universes out there.

These are faith positions without evidence.

Atheism asks us to believe in an infinite number of metaphysical realities for which we have no evidence, but Christianity asks us to believe in one: God, for which we have an enormous amount of evidence.

—MARK CLARK

The evidence points toward the existence of God.

Group Discussion

Take a few minutes with your group members to discuss what you just watched and explore these concepts in Scripture. Then take time to pray together as a group. Use the space at the end of this session to keep track of prayer requests and group updates.

1. What stood out to you from Mark's teaching on the problem of God's existence?

2. Have you ever doubted God's existence or questioned the creation of the universe? Why or why not?

3. **Read Romans 2:12–16.** According to the apostle Paul, where does our inner moral law come from? How do you know this to be true for you?

4. How does science point to the evidence of God?

5. **Read Job 11:7–9.** What mystery remains for us as a human race, and for you as an individual, regarding the existence of God and the creation of the universe?

6. Mark said, *"It takes more faith to believe that our universe came into existence out of nothing rather than the belief that someone created it."* How does this statement of faith influence the way you understand the existence of God and the universe?

_____

_____

_____

Pray

Pray as a group before you close your time together. Thank God for the evidence that allows us to trust the universe as it points to the existence of God. Ask God to continue to open your mind to the reasoning and the mystery behind God's existence and the creation of the universe. May we have the simple faith that it takes to believe God is real and present with us in this beautifully created and ever-expanding universe we call home. Use this space to keep track of prayer requests and group updates.

_____

_____

_____

_____

_____

_____

_____

_____

_____

_____

_____

_____

_____

_____

Between-Sessions
PERSONAL STUDY

Weekly Reflection

Before you begin the between-sessions exercises, briefly review your video notes for session 2. In the space below, write down the *most significant point* you took away from this session.

_____

_____

_____

_____

Take some time to reflect on the material you covered during your group time by engaging in any or all of the following between-sessions exercises. As you read and experience the material, you may want to make a few notes in your guide. The primary goal of these activities is for your own spiritual growth and personal reflection, and they are not a requirement for group participation. If you haven't done so already, read chapter two in *The Problem of God*.

Day 1: People as Evidence for God
Read: *Romans 2:12–16; James 1*

Consider: Have you ever watched or listened to children playing with one another out on the playground, in a classroom, or among the stash of games and toys at home? If you stop and listen for just sixty seconds, I guarantee you'll hear some version of the law of morality. "It's my turn on the trampoline; you already had your turn," or "I cleaned up the toys yesterday; it's your turn to clean them up today." At some point you're bound to hear someone cry out, "But that's not fair!" Children at play are constantly appealing to an unspoken, yet agreed upon, understanding of the universe. Deep down inside they believe there is an objective standard of fairness and that we should all "follow the rules."

But have you ever stopped to think about who told them about these rules? Maybe it was you, or the hovering parent from next door, or the strict teacher across the hallway, but the truth for most kids is, *no one told them the rules.* No one had to. They were predisposed to believe them. This moral law is built within them, and of course, this does not just pertain to children, but to all of us. No matter how old we are or what language we speak, we can all agree on the dos and don'ts of moral law. Someone must have decided at some point that cutting in line is wrong, and this moral law has been hardwired into us as human beings ever since—a reality that separates us from animals.

But where did we get this transcendent view of morality that spans across all cultures and time? When did we all agree on these foundational morals? Christianity says our morals came from God. If there is a moral law, then there must be a moral *lawgiver.* The existence of our moral convictions points to the existence of God, who placed within us a moral law including the love of all people and the passion to lay down our lives for the good of others. Our moral law is what it means to have the heart of God stitched into our being.

Reflect: Take a few moments to reflect on your answers to these questions.

Name a few examples of universal moral laws.

_____

_____

_____

What specific things cause you to think about these universal moral laws—situations or circumstances of love and grace or injustice or lack of fairness?

_____

_____

_____

According to these passages, how does the idea of universal moral laws reveal and reflect the existence of God?

_____

_____

_____

Pray: Close out your time today by praying to God regarding his existence present in our universal moral laws. May you see God every time you notice a moral law from within.

Day 2: The Universe as Evidence for God
Read: *Colossians 1:15–20; Hebrews 11:1–3; Revelation 4:11*

Consider: Many people have attempted to deny that cosmological evidence leads to God even though science now concludes that the universe has a birthday. The universe began to exist fifteen billion years ago, and we know that whatever begins to exist has a cause. While there are some who cling to the "nothing hypothesis"—the idea that the universe came into existence in a big bang out of nothing—it doesn't take a genius to realize that this explanation doesn't work scientifically, philosophically, or experientially.

"Nothing" is what tired people say; people who want to go back to "sleep," people who want you to stop asking questions. But something caused the big bang existence of the universe—when all space, matter, energy, even time itself, began to exist at some point in the past. And if something begins to exist, then its existence is dependent on something outside of it that preexisted it, causing it to come into being. This is called "contingency." Thanks to Edwin Hubble who discovered in 1929 that the universe itself actually began to exist, we have the big bang theory.

This event, however it happened, is what Genesis calls "the beginning" (Genesis 1:1). God created the universe, starting with light and moving from there (Genesis 1:3). The big bang points to divine design. Only a supernatural force outside of space and time could have created nature because nature could not create itself. And this divine design points to a divine designer: God.

Reflect: Take a few moments to reflect on your answers to these questions.

Have you ever considered the big bang theory as the same event as creation? Why or why not?

_____

_____

_____

Now that you are examining how your view of science influences your perspective of God's existence, is there anything new that stands out to you about the original creation story found in Genesis?

_____

_____

_____

How do the authors of the other passages in this session point to the universe as evidence for the existence of God?

_____

_____

_____

Pray: Close out your time today by praying to God about God's existence as displayed through the creation of the universe. May you delight in noticing God's existence in new ways.

Day 3: The Struggle to Believe
Read: *Jeremiah 10:11–13; John 1:1–5 and 4:23–24; 2 Peter 3:1–9*

Consider: If you're struggling to believe the evidence regarding the existence of God, then the onus is on you for proving God's nonexistence. This is not as easy as it seems. When we reject the existence of God, we create more moral, philosophical, and scientific problems than we solve. To believe something, we must present counterevidence. True, we have no evidence that God ever *began* to exist, but we have evidence that the universe began to exist.

So, what are the options if we don't want to believe in God despite the counterevidence? There's the "lucky us" theory which states, "Lucky us! The universe just happened to come into existence." Or there's the "multiverse" theory which states that our universe is one of many universes coexisting like bubbles of foam in a "multiverse," but this theory doesn't hold up under scrutiny either. These theories are actually faith positions that lack evidence and belong to the realm of pure conjecture.

It's ironic that in the end, atheism asks us to believe in an infinite number of metaphysical realities with no evidence, while Christianity asks us to believe in one (God) for which we do actually have evidence in the divine design of the universe. If you're struggling to believe, consider that it's more rational to believe in the existence of God than not.

Reflect: Take a few moments to reflect on your answers to these questions.

Are you still struggling to believe in the existence of God? Why or why not?

_____

_____

_____

How do these passages make a strong case for God's existence and the divine design of the universe?

_____

_____

_____

What remaining questions do you have about the existence of God? Write them down here, and share them with your pastor, a trusted mentor, a friend, or your small group for this study.

_____

_____

_____

Pray: Close out your time today by praying to God about whatever it is you're struggling to believe about God, his existence, or the creation of the universe. May you begin to see the existence of God as you pay attention to the world around you.

For Next Week: Read chapter three in *The Problem of God* and use the space below to write any insights or questions from your personal study that you want to discuss at the next group meeting.

Journal, Reflections, and Notes

_____

_____

_____

_____

_____

_____

_____

_____

_____

_____

_____

_____

The Problem of
THE BIBLE

*"I will put my law in their minds
and write it on their hearts."*

—JEREMIAH 31:33

Welcome

As a young man, I believed in Christ before I ever entered a church. My encounter with God was primarily with the Bible itself, not with Christians or the church at all. I would sit at local parks or out in front of my high school, smoking half a pack of cigarettes and devouring the Bible. I read the stories of Jesus and his teachings and I took them to heart.

Over time, faith grew within me, and I started to believe and change. I went from stealing cars, throwing rocks through people's windows, and doing drugs, to becoming a seventeen-year-old young man who loved God and, because of that love, was lit on fire to change the world. I was living a new kind of existence, but not because a church told me to, or leaders were discipling me, or my parents were guiding me; it was because of the Bible itself, or because of God *through* the Bible—the Word behind the word—changing me.

I took the teachings of Jesus to heart and believed that Jesus died to liberate me from myself so that I could live for him. This is the power of the Bible. If we listen to the Scriptures and heed their instruction, they will transform us forever. In order to trust the Bible to the point where it can transform our lives, we must explore its accuracy, its trustworthiness, and its truthfulness.

Share

If you or any of your group members are just getting to know one another, take a few minutes to introduce yourselves. Then, to kick things off, briefly discuss one of the following:

- Name a few critiques you've heard about the credibility of the Bible.

  —or—

- If you were face-to-face with Jesus and could ask him a question about the Bible, what would it be?

Read 📖

Invite someone to read aloud the following passage as preparation for Mark's teaching. Listen for fresh insights as you hear the verses being read, and then briefly discuss the questions that follow.

PSALM 119:1–35

Blessed are those whose ways are blameless,
    who walk according to the law of the LORD.
Blessed are those who keep his statutes
    and seek him with all their heart—
they do no wrong
    but follow his ways.
You have laid down precepts
    that are to be fully obeyed.
Oh, that my ways were steadfast
    in obeying your decrees!
Then I would not be put to shame
    when I consider all your commands.
I will praise you with an upright heart
    as I learn your righteous laws.
I will obey your decrees;
    do not utterly forsake me.

How can a young person stay on the path of purity?
>By living according to your word.

I seek you with all my heart;
>do not let me stray from your commands.

I have hidden your word in my heart
>that I might not sin against you.

Praise be to you, LORD;
>teach me your decrees.

With my lips I recount
>all the laws that come from your mouth.

I rejoice in following your statutes
>as one rejoices in great riches.

I meditate on your precepts
>and consider your ways.

I delight in your decrees;
>I will not neglect your word.

Be good to your servant while I live,
>that I may obey your word.

Open my eyes that I may see
>wonderful things in your law.

I am a stranger on earth;
>do not hide your commands from me.

My soul is consumed with longing
>for your laws at all times.

You rebuke the arrogant, who are accursed,
>those who stray from your commands.

Remove from me their scorn and contempt,
>for I keep your statutes.

Though rulers sit together and slander me,
>your servant will meditate on your decrees.

Your statutes are my delight;
>they are my counselors.

I am laid low in the dust;

    preserve my life according to your word.

I gave an account of my ways and you answered me;

    teach me your decrees.

Cause me to understand the way of your precepts,

    that I may meditate on your wonderful deeds.

My soul is weary with sorrow;

    strengthen me according to your word.

Keep me from deceitful ways;

    be gracious to me and teach me your law.

I have chosen the way of faithfulness;

    I have set my heart on your laws.

I hold fast to your statutes, LORD;

    do not let me be put to shame.

I run in the path of your commands,

    for you have broadened my understanding.

Teach me, LORD, the way of your decrees,

    that I may follow it to the end.

Give me understanding, so that I may keep your law

    and obey it with all my heart.

Direct me in the path of your commands,

    for there I find delight.

What new insight do you notice in this passage?

_____

_____

_____

Consider as you listen to Mark's teaching, *how do you reflect the credibility of the Bible in the way you live your life?*

_____

_____

_____

Watch ▶

Play the video segment for session 3. As you watch, use the following outline to record any thoughts or concepts that stand out to you.

NOTES

——— The Legitimacy of the Bible ———

Is it accurate?
Is it trustworthy?
Is it true and reliable?

> Tell a devout Christian that his wife is cheating on him, or that frozen yogurt can make a man invisible, he's likely to require as much evidence as everyone else. Tell him that the book he keeps by his bedside was written by an invisible deity who will punish him with fire for eternity if he fails to accept its very incredible claim about the Universe and he seems to require no evidence whatsoever.
>
> —SAM HARRIS

——— Digging into the Claims of the Bible ———

Key Question: How did Jesus respond when his own disciples had questions like this?

1. **General and Special Revelation:** God has spoken to humankind in different ways. Creation is a *general revelation.*

> For since the creation of the world God's invisible qualities—his eternal power and divine nature—have been clearly seen, being understood from what has been made, so that people are without excuse.
>
> —ROMANS 1:20

The Bible is a *special revelation*—it is a written account through human authors inspired by the Holy Spirit.

2. **The Bible as a good story and as history:** many people respect it as a good story, but they don't consider it good history.

——— Common Questions about the Bible ———

1. Has the Bible changed? The answer is no.

> Historians tell us the Bible is one of the most, if not the most, reliable and credible documents from antiquity.
> —MARK CLARK

> *The evidence:* copies of the ancient texts are similar according to the scribes.

2. Is the Bible full of contradictions and mistakes? The answer is no.
   The evidence: contradictions are not true errors but passages that are misread or misunderstood and have been explained by scholars for many years; there are small variations according to language.
   The two most disputed passages: Mark 16:9–20 and John 7:53–8:11.
   Case Studies on Biblical Contradictions:

> We are demanding a level of precision and perfection that we don't demand of other forms of ancient literature, of any sort of literature from that time at all.
> —MARK CLARK

> Old Testament vs. New Testament.
> There are different eras in salvation history.

> "Behold, the days are coming, declares the LORD, . . . [when] I will put my law within them, and I will write it on their hearts. And I will be their God, and they shall be my people."
> —JEREMIAH 31:31, 33 ESV

The law of the Old Testament was given for a season of salvation history until the Spirit of God comes to live within our lives, our bodies. The laws point to the fullness of Jesus. Jesus ushers in a whole new era of salvation history.

3. Can we trust the Bible culturally and personally?

Tim Keller, the author of *The Reason for God*, identifies other problems skeptics have for trusting the Bible.

The Cultural Disconnect: Consider the idea that the Bible might not always be teaching what you think it might be teaching. We have to understand its context.

For example: Slavery.

> Slaves, obey your earthly masters in everything.
>
> —COLOSSIANS 3:22

Roman slavery in the first century was different than our understanding of slavery today.

85–90% of the inhabitants of Rome and Italy were actually slaves or of slave origin in the first and second centuries AD. Slaves enjoyed great popularity in Rome. They were the trusted household servants, teachers, librarians, accountants, and estate managers. And because slavery was a form of employment, you could work your way out of slavery.

> —A. A. RUPRECHT

Paul's advice for slaves in Colossians 3: *work hard and respect your superiors.*

For example: Ways of Living and Acting in Society.

Two primary ways of living in the Old Testament: Polygamy and Primogeniture

When you read the book of Genesis, you begin to realize that God is overthrowing both of these institutions. He's challenging polygamy and he's challenging primogeniture in a very interesting way.

> —MARK CLARK

For example: The Pool at Bethesda (John 5).

It may be stated categorically that no archaeological discovery has ever contradicted a biblical reference.

> —NELSON GLUECK, JEWISH ARCHAEOLOGIST

Don't reject the Bible based on your cultural understanding. Take the time to learn what the Bible is actually saying.

The Personal Trust: people reject the Bible because of what it personally demands of them.

Jesus challenges this way of relating to God.

They asked each other, "Were not our hearts burning within us while he talked with us on the road and opened the Scriptures to us?"

—LUKE 24:32

Every story whispers his name.

—*THE JESUS STORYBOOK BIBLE*

The message of the Bible is about what Jesus has done.

[The Bible is] the face of God for us now.

—AUGUSTINE

Scripture reveals the person and the work of Jesus to us in a way that is absolutely trustworthy in every way.

Group Discussion

Take a few minutes with your group members to discuss what you just watched and explore these concepts in Scripture. Then take time to pray together as a group. Use the space at the end of this session to keep track of prayer requests and group updates.

1. What stood out to you from Mark's teaching on the problem of the Bible?

_____

_____

_____

2. Have you ever questioned the credibility or the validity of the Bible? What caused these questions or doubts for you?

_____

_____

_____

3. **Read 2 Timothy 3:16–17.** How does the apostle Paul explain Scripture, and what does he mean by this description?

_____

_____

_____

4. In what ways has your Bible equipped you for "good work" (2 Timothy 3:17) or for living a "good life"? And how does your experience of the Bible deepen or expand its credibility for you?

_____

_____

_____

5. **Read Jeremiah 31:31–34.** How does the Old Testament point to the person and the work of Jesus?

_____

_____

_____

6. What does Augustine mean when he refers to the Bible as the "face of God for us now"? How has this been true for you?

_____

_____

_____

Pray

Pray as a group before you close your time together. Thank God for the trustworthy credibility of the Bible. Ask God for wisdom and understanding regarding the cultural disconnect we may experience or feel today. May we have eyes to see beyond the cultural disconnection as we learn more about the context, and may we have hearts that place a personal faith and trust in the Bible as it points to Jesus. Use this space to keep track of prayer requests and group updates.

Between-Sessions
PERSONAL STUDY

Weekly Reflection

Before you begin the between-sessions exercises, briefly review your video notes for session 3. In the space below, write down the *most significant point* you took away from this session.

_____

_____

_____

_____

Take some time to reflect on the material you covered during your group time by engaging in any or all of the following between-sessions exercises. As you read and experience the material, you may want to make a few notes in your guide. The primary goal of these activities is for your own spiritual growth and personal reflection, and they are not a requirement for group participation. If you haven't done so already, read chapter three in *The Problem of God*.

Day 1: Has the Bible Been Changed?
Read: *Luke 24:13–27; Hebrews 11*

Consider: People often criticize Christians for blindly believing the Bible. But the Christians that I know aren't just blindly believing it, they are digging into the evidence of the Bible's claims. They want to know the historical reliability of the Bible, and that it aligns with archaeology and science rather than ancient mythology and fairy tales. That's why it's important to note that modern-day historians tell us that the Bible is one of the most reliable and credible documents from ancient history.

One of the reasons it remains so credible to this day is that it has largely remained the same throughout history. The ancient Jewish scribes who wrote both the Old and New Testaments had a deep passion for preserving the purity and accuracy of all of what they considered to be "authoritative texts," making sure these texts were not changed in any significant way through the passing of time. For this very reason, the scribes—a particular class of biblical scholars—would make copies of biblical books by handwriting chapters and chapters of the text so the original manuscripts were preserved in the new copies. One scribe would write, while two other scribes stood over his shoulders as he worked. If the first scribe made an error, they would correct the mistake, then all three would have to initial the correction as it was being copied or the manuscript would be destroyed. This was an extremely laborious process that took a great deal of time and attention.

For this reason, you can compare two copies of the same passage copied five hundred years apart in completely different geographical areas, and they will be virtually identical. This is the credibility of the Scriptures we have today.

Reflect: Take a few moments to reflect on your answers to these questions.

Why do you think the disciples doubted the appearance of Jesus, even when they knew the Old Testament prophecies about him?

_____

_____

_____

Hebrews 11 is often referred to as the "Hall of Faith." How does this list reinforce the historical credibility of the Bible?

_____

_____

_____

How do you answer the questions and statements of skeptics who insist the Bible has changed over time?

_____

_____

_____

Pray: Close out your time today by praying to God as you consider the careful preservation and historical credibility of the Bible. May the reliability and accuracy of the Bible ring true to you.

Day 2: Is the Bible Full of Contradictions?
Read: *Mark 16:9–20; John 7:53–8:11; 2 Timothy 3:14–17*

Consider: Sadly, the skeptical claim that the Bible contains contradictions and historical mistakes has caused many Christians to doubt their faith and many skeptics to feel justified in their assertions of errors in the Bible. But the mistakes people commonly cite in the Bible are nothing new. If we take a close look at the context of what skeptics claimed to be "thousands of mistakes" in the Bible, what we really see are small variations between different manuscripts. In other words, the mistakes aren't really mistakes at all; they are simply places in the text where a word is spelled differently or used differently in the original Greek or Hebrew between manuscripts.

These slight variations are not scattered equally throughout the New Testament but clustered in certain areas. It's also important to understand that there are only two disputed passages in the entire New Testament—Mark 16:9–20 and John 7:53–8:11—and those passages are labeled as such in English versions of the Bible either in a footnote or in the actual passage, saying: "The earliest manuscripts do not include this passage." So, the next time you have your own questions about contradictions in the Bible, or you hear someone else claiming there are thousands of mistakes, lean in to examine the text and ask questions. Ask yourself and others, "Was this seeming contradiction truly a mistake, or is it simply a slight variation in wording or spelling?"

Reflect: Take a few moments to reflect on your answers to these questions.

What stands out to you about the way these disputed passages are noted in your Bible? Why are these passages disputed?

_____

_____

_____

How does the apostle Paul describe Scripture in 2 Timothy, and why was this so significant?

_____

_____

_____

Have you ever told the same story in different settings with details slightly different based on your audience? What was the story, and what were the circumstances for sharing?

_____

_____

_____

Pray: Close out your time today by praying to God about this idea of contradictions in the Bible. May you learn to accept the truth of the Bible even with slight variations in the text.

Day 3: Is the Bible Trustworthy?
Read: *Colossians 2:6–17; Acts 10; Galatians 3:10–14*

Consider: Another common question about the Bible is whether or not it's trustworthy. Some people cite the differences between the Old Testament and the New Testament as proof it's not a trustworthy text. And yet what we see when we experience the Bible as a whole is that we can't understand the Bible without understanding it as a progressive story. The Law of the Old Testament was given for a season of salvation history, one that would eventually give way to another season: one in which the Spirit of God would come to live in individual people, empowering them to be obedient to him in all things.

The Bible is a progressive revelation that reveals the truth about God to us, not in a static way but in progressive stages, and the latter stages overshadow and leave behind the former stages. Christians no longer live under the rules of the kingdom of Israel but under the rule of Jesus in his new kingdom, and under the events of Jesus bringing his new kingdom to earth through his life, ministry, miracles, death, and resurrection. These events are *public historical events recorded by an actual audience with real names.* When we understand the historical and cultural context of the Bible—the way it used culturally appropriate methods to challenge the status quo—we can trust the Bible as it progressively points to Jesus.

Some of us may have a lot of hang-ups about the Bible and the way it was used as a threat or a burden in our homes growing up or in our faith communities. But the truth is, the Bible isn't about you or me; it's not about what we can do so God will love and save us. The Bible is about what Jesus has done. It's about who he is and what he has done for all of humanity, including me and you. And that's why we can consider the Bible trustworthy.

Reflect: Take a few moments to reflect on your answers to these questions.

How is the Bible historically and culturally trustworthy from your perspective?

_____

_____

_____

How has the Bible become personally trustworthy to you?

_____

_____

_____

What do these passages tell us about the progressive nature of the salvation story of the Bible?

_____

_____

_____

Pray: Close out your time today by praying to God about the trustworthiness of the Bible.

For Next Week: Read chapter four in *The Problem of God* and use the space below to write any insights or questions from your personal study that you want to discuss at the next group meeting.

Journal, Reflections, and Notes

_____

_____

_____

_____

_____

_____

The Problem of
THE CHRIST MYTH

These are a shadow of the things that were to come; the reality, however, is found in Christ.

—COLOSSIANS 2:17

Welcome

I'll never forget the day my neighbor told me he respected me and the work I do as a pastor, but he believed it was all based on a lie—that Jesus never really existed. I was a bit surprised by this interaction, so I asked him to explain what he meant. As he began to unpack his thoughts, he described what has become known today as the Christ Myth, and it was as though he were reading the "Christ Myth" script. He said Jesus was a fictional character of history, not a real human; and that he was modeled after mythological gods whose stories predate Jesus by thousands of years. People who believe this extremely popular Christ Myth view today insist the church invented Jesus, and that there are other existing myths about gods that heal people, walk on water, feed thousands, have twelve disciples, then die and rise again after three days of being buried in the ground. He believed the existence of these other myths was proof that Jesus was modeled after them. As my neighbor would say, people who believe the Christ Myth believe that Christianity was the greatest story ever *sold*, not just the greatest story ever told. There are even books and movies to support this popular challenge to Christianity.

But the Christ Myth falls apart with just a small amount of historical study. When you look closely, the facts are misinterpreted and skewed to force parallels with Christianity. The two most credible disputes to the Christ Myth are the actual first-century accounts from historians and writers outside the Bible, as well as one of the greatest anomalies of history, the rise of the early church after the death of Jesus. And as we will explore today, it's hard to argue with the credibility of historical facts.

Share 💬

To kick things off, briefly discuss one of the following:

- Name one or two of the greatest myths of all time.

  —or—

- How do you respond to people who say Jesus was a fictional character, not a real person?

Read 📖

Invite someone to read aloud the following passage as preparation for Mark's teaching. Listen for fresh insights as you hear the verses being read, and then briefly discuss the questions that follow.

ISAIAH 53

> Who has believed our message
>> and to whom has the arm of the LORD been revealed?
> He grew up before him like a tender shoot,
>> and like a root out of dry ground.
> He had no beauty or majesty to attract us to him,
>> nothing in his appearance that we should desire him.
> He was despised and rejected by mankind,
>> a man of suffering, and familiar with pain.
> Like one from whom people hide their faces
>> he was despised, and we held him in low esteem.
>
> Surely he took up our pain
>> and bore our suffering,
> yet we considered him punished by God,
>> stricken by him, and afflicted.

But he was pierced for our transgressions,
>   he was crushed for our iniquities;
the punishment that brought us peace was on him,
>   and by his wounds we are healed.
We all, like sheep, have gone astray,
>   each of us has turned to our own way;
and the LORD has laid on him
>   the iniquity of us all.

He was oppressed and afflicted,
>   yet he did not open his mouth;
he was led like a lamb to the slaughter,
>   and as a sheep before its shearers is silent,
>   so he did not open his mouth.
By oppression and judgment he was taken away.
>   Yet who of his generation protested?
For he was cut off from the land of the living;
>   for the transgression of my people he was punished.
He was assigned a grave with the wicked,
>   and with the rich in his death,
though he had done no violence,
>   nor was any deceit in his mouth.

Yet it was the LORD's will to crush him and cause him to suffer,
>   and though the LORD makes his life an offering for sin,
he will see his offspring and prolong his days,
>   and the will of the LORD will prosper in his hand.
After he has suffered,
>   he will see the light of life and be satisfied;
by his knowledge my righteous servant will justify many,
>   and he will bear their iniquities.
Therefore I will give him a portion among the great,
>   and he will divide the spoils with the strong,

because he poured out his life unto death,

and was numbered with the transgressors.

For he bore the sin of many,

and made intercession for the transgressors.

What new insight do you notice in this passage?

_____

_____

_____

Consider as you listen to Mark's teaching, *how do stories and prophecies of ancient history point to the truth revealed in Jesus Christ?*

_____

_____

_____

Watch ▶

Play the video segment for session 4. As you watch, use the following outline to record any thoughts or concepts that stand out to you.

NOTES

—— Jesus and the Myths of Ancient Gods ——

The historical context: The first modern attempt to deny Jesus occurred in the eighteenth century.

According to this attempt, Christianity was simply an "amalgamation" of various ancient mythologies. Jesus was constructed by the early Church as another mythological character.

Scholars debate:

- The nature of Jesus
- The exact date of his birth
- What he did
- What he taught

But scholars affirm that Jesus existed.

> I'm a historian, I'm not a believer. But I must confess as a historian, that the penniless preacher from Nazareth is irrevocably the very center of history. Jesus Christ is easily the most dominant figure in all history.
>
> —H. G. WELLS

Buzz Aldrin: The second man on the Moon.

> There is more proof for the existence of Jesus than any other founder of a major religion in history.
>
> —MARK CLARK

The Popular Claim about the Christ Myth:

> Jesus Christ is a mythical character based on various ubiquitous god-men and universal saviors who were part of the ancient world for thousands of years prior to the Christian era.
>
> —WALTER P. WEAVER, *THE HISTORICAL JESUS IN THE TWENTIETH CENTURY*

——— The Current Presentation of the Christ Myth ———

People attempt to demonstrate strict and precise parallels between Jesus and other mythological figures in the following areas:

- They had twelve disciples.
- They were born of a virgin on December 25.
- There were visited by Magi after the birth.
- They did miracles.
- Their disciples were persecuted.
- They died and were resurrected after three days.

Key Question: How do we respond to the Christ Myth narratives?

———— The Historical Study of Jesus ————

1. *Did Jesus really exist?*

   The evidence: At least ten writers outside of the Bible mention Jesus by name—they were first-century historians, Jewish and Roman.

   The persecution of the early Church is crucial evidence of the existence of Jesus.

2. *Did Jesus really rise from the dead?*

   The rise of the early Church is crucial evidence for the resurrection of Jesus.

———— The Problems of the Christ Myth ————

The primary sources of the myth did not interact with the primary sources they claim to be parallels to Christianity.

> Horus had twelve disciples and it was upon this fact that the Gospel writers modeled Jesus' twelve disciples.
>
> —ACHARYA S.

> The Christ Myth loses credibility because it gets the facts wrong about both the ancient myths and Christianity, itself.
>
> —MARK CLARK

An example of the false: The *Zeitgeist* movie and the symbolic number twelve.

An example of the truth: Horus was a fisherman and had four disciples, all of whom were listed as animals.

> Over and over again, the facts are misinterpreted and skewed to force parallels with Christianity.
>
> —MARK CLARK

Key Questions: Are there any direct parallels between Jesus Christ and these popular ancient gods? And if so, does Christianity crumble under the weight of the Christ Myth?

———— **The Parallels of the Christ Myth** ————

THE CLAIMS ABOUT HORUS	THE HISTORICAL ACCOUNTS OF HORUS
• He was born of a virgin on December 25 • He was born in a manger • Three kings followed a star to his location • He was a child teacher by the age of twelve • He was baptized in a river by Anup, who was later beheaded • He had twelve disciples • He was a fisherman • He was crucified between two thieves • He was raised from the dead three days later	• Mother, Isis, and father, Osiris, and their conception story • Horus's birthdate varies; Jesus was not born on December 25 • No one spoke of the three kings following a star until the 19th century; Christianity never claims three kings were present at the birth of Jesus (Matthew 2) • Horus did not die, or if he did, he was cut up by an enemy and thrown into the water, then fished out by crocodiles. This is not a resurrection parallel.

And so on with the incredible myths and parallels of other deities:

• Mithras
• Dionysus

There are no parallels with Christianity in these myths. Several of the myths actually borrow details from Christianity.

Parallelomania: *example of the lives and stories of JFK and Abraham Lincoln*

Key Question: What do we do with these myths that predate Jesus?

JOHN F. KENNEDY	ABRAHAM LINCOLN

They show that what the law requires is written on their hearts, while their conscience also bears witness and their conflicting thoughts accuse or perhaps excuse them on that day when, according to my gospel, God judges the secrets of men by Christ Jesus.

—ROMANS 2:15–16 RSV

This very thing, which is now called the Christian religion, existed before. It was not absent from the beginning of the human race until Christ came in the flesh, but it was then that the true religion that already existed began to be called "Christian."

—AUGUSTINE

Pre-Christian Christianity: *A Cruciform pattern stitched into the fabric of human history.*

These are only a shadow of what is to come; but the substance belongs to Christ.

—COLOSSIANS 2:17 RSV

God used stories and myths to prepare humankind to hear and understand the gospel. The conversation between J. R. R. Tolkien and C. S. Lewis:

Just as speech is invention about objects and ideas, so myth is invention about truth. We have come from God, and inevitably the myths woven by us, though they contain error, will also reflect a splintered fragment of the true light, the eternal truth that is with God. Our myths may be misguided, but they steer, however shakily, towards the true harbor.

—J. R. R. TOLKIEN

The critical difference between mythical stories and the gospel, according to Tolkien: *What the gospel said was actually true.*

It was fairy-story incarnate; legend and history meeting as one.

—J. R. R. TOLKIEN

The old myth of the dying God comes down from the heaven of legend and imagination to the Earth of history. It happens. At a particular date in a particular place, from Osiris dying, and nobody knows when or where, to a historical person crucified. It's all in order, under Pontius Pilate. Christ is more than Osiris, not less. We must not be ashamed of the parallels; they ought to be there. It would be a stumbling block if they weren't. Those who do not know that this great myth became fact when the virgin conceived are indeed to be pitied.

—C. S. LEWIS

God gives us stories and experiences that lead us to the person and work of Jesus. The story of your life is God's way of leading you to know him.

The challenge: *Take the confrontation of history and the challenge of Jesus and ask: What am I supposed to do with this person? Am I going to deny his draw or am I going to surrender to it?*

Group Discussion

Take a few minutes with your group members to discuss what you just watched and explore these concepts in Scripture. Then take time to pray together as a group. Use the space at the end of this session to keep track of prayer requests and group updates.

1. What stood out to you from Mark's teaching on the problem of the Christ Myth?

   _____

   _____

   _____

2. Have you ever before heard these questions or doubts about Jesus as the Christ? How will you respond to these questions and doubts based on what you learned today?

   _____

   _____

   _____

3. Consider the idea of parallelism. Are there other parallels made between modern-day people or myths and the story of Jesus—in movies, books, the news, even in church culture? Why are these parallels significant today?

_____

_____

_____

4. **Read Luke 7:24–30 and Matthew 11:7–15.** What are the parallels found in these passages, and other places in the Bible, regarding Jesus and John the Baptist?

_____

_____

_____

5. **Read Colossians 2.** How do the apostle Paul's warnings and encouragement to the Colossians stand true for us today, especially as it relates to the Christ Myth?

_____

_____

_____

6. How have myths served, as J. R. R. Tolkien says, to "steer us towards the true harbor" of the truth in Christ? And how can we hold space for myths and truth as we practice our Christian faith?

_____

_____

_____

Pray

Pray as a group before you close your time together. Thank God for the creativity of myths throughout time that "point to splintered fragments of the true light," as J. R. R. Tolkien said. Ask God for wisdom and understanding regarding the cultural myths we've experienced and listened to over the years of our lives. May we have eyes to see beyond the myths and parallels of ancient and modern-day stories as they point to the truth of God and the credibility of Jesus Christ. Use this space to keep track of prayer requests and group updates.

Between-Sessions
PERSONAL STUDY

Weekly Reflection

Before you begin the between-sessions exercises, briefly review your video notes for session 4. In the space below, write down the *most significant point* you took away from this session.

_____

_____

_____

_____

Take some time to reflect on the material you covered during your group time by engaging in any or all of the following between-sessions exercises. As you read and experience the material, you may want to make a few notes in your guide. The primary goal of these activities is for your own spiritual growth and personal reflection, and they are not a requirement for group participation. If you haven't done so already, read chapter four in *The Problem of God*.

Day 1: The Story of the Magi
Read: *Matthew 2; Daniel 5*

Consider: The Christ Myth loses credibility because it gets the facts wrong, not only about ancient myths but about Christianity itself. This happens for several reasons, one being the proponents of the myth rarely interact with the primary sources of Christianity, namely the Gospels themselves as well as the ancient texts containing the most popular myths that hold loose parallels to the life and death of Jesus.

Take for instance the parallel of the "three kings"—mentioned in astrology, in myth, and in the story of Jesus. This concept of the celestial "three kings" came from the constellation Orion in which there is a lead star and three other main stars that all make up the astrological feature called Orion's Belt. The three stars in the constellation are commonly called the "three kings." There's a popular belief that the three stars follow the lead star to the birth of a cosmic savior, and skeptics argue that the story of Jesus and the Magi reflect this astrology in myth. But it would be impossible for the Gospel writers to base their story on this astrological idea because the story hadn't even been invented until the nineteenth century.

If we look closely at the Gospel records of Jesus and the Magi, we see that Christianity never claims there were *three kings* present at the birth of Jesus—only an unnamed, unnumbered group of Magi who brought three presents to Jesus, who was most likely a toddler in his home, not a baby in his manger. And the Magi were not kings; they were Babylonian or Persian astrologers and magicians as we read about in Daniel 5. So, the idea that the story of Jesus and the Magi is simply a mythological reflection of the astrological occurrence of Orion's Belt doesn't stack up to the historical evidence and Gospel claims.

Reflect: Take a few moments to reflect on your answers to these questions.

What does Matthew 2 tell you about the Magi?

_____

_____

_____

What do you learn about the Babylonian Magi in Daniel 5? How does this passage illuminate your understanding of the Magi in the Gospel of Matthew?

_____

_____

_____

Is the evidence enough to make you believe in the visit between the Magi and Jesus as an actual, historical event rather than a myth based on an astrological occurrence? Why or why not?

_____

_____

_____

Pray: Close out your time today by praying that God will make the historical evidence of Jesus real to you. May you find the historical Jesus to be true.

Day 2: Parallelomania
Read: *1 Timothy 1:1–7; 1 Timothy 4; 2 Timothy 4:1–8*

Consider: Christianity does not claim to be the first religion to speak of the concept of gods becoming human, dying, and then being resurrected—in a general sense. There are other stories and other religious beliefs rooted in these stories that share these themes. But the similarity in the details between these pagan religions and Christianity are few, with very loose connections. Several of these myths actually come later than Christianity and borrow from Christianity, rather than the other way around. But what do we do about the parallels and loose connections that *predate* Christ? Well, it's like we talked about in the teaching session. No one questions the existence of John F. Kennedy because he came after Abraham Lincoln, even though their lives shared *many* uncanny parallels. There is simply no legitimate connection between the lives and deaths of these two men. In the same way, it's not reasonable to question the life and death of Jesus even if there are parallels of his life and death with other mythological figures. Perhaps these parallels between Jesus and other gods were God's intentional plan. Jesus shatters all other myths with the historical and credible details of his death and resurrection. Maybe we wouldn't be able to recognize this life-transforming, history-altering moment if it didn't resemble something we were familiar with in the stories we know about human history.

Reflect: Take a few moments to reflect on your answers to these questions.

What stands out to you about the way Paul warns of false teachers and false doctrines in these passages?

_____

_____

_____

What does Paul mean in 1 Timothy 1:5 when he says "the goal of this command is love"?

_____

_____

_____

Why do you think we are drawn to "godless myths and old wives' tales" (1 Timothy 4:7) even when we know the truth about Jesus? What myths or tales have caused you to doubt your faith in the past?

_____

_____

_____

Pray: Close out your time today by praying to God about the temptation to see other myths or even other true stories as credible parallels to Jesus. May you see the credible truth of Jesus as the one true story of God.

Day 3: The True Myth
Read: *Romans 2:12–16; Colossians 2:16–17; 1 Corinthians 15:3–49*

Consider: When we try to force parallels between Christianity and pagan stories, we run the danger of minimizing the differences. But there is danger in the opposite as well. Myths have their place in human history as expressions of a deep yearning in our consciousness. And the deep yearning of humanity has been for God to come into intimate contact with us, repair the damage made by sin, and give us safety and security that lasts forever. And this is exactly what God has done. In other words, we told ourselves these stories in myths, until they became true in Jesus.

The miraculous births, adventures, heroes, and happy endings *actually happened* in the gospel. Christianity became the best of both worlds in Jesus—the fairy-story incarnate, and legend and history meeting as one (in the paraphrased words of J. R. R. Tolkien). It was through rationale that God's existence was understood, and through the imagination that God's significance was understood. This kind of worldview that included the story of Christ gave life *more* meaning, adventure, and romance, not less. And the preceding stories and myths of Christianity were shadows, and as C. S. Lewis wrote, these shadows were "anticipation of the full truth." This is the rationale and the romanticism of the true myth of Jesus Christ.

Reflect: Take a few moments to reflect on your answers to these questions.

According to Paul, how do people show "the requirements of the law are written on their hearts" (Romans 2:15)? Why is it important for both the Jews and Gentiles in Paul's audience to hear him say this?

_____

_____

_____

What is Paul referring to by "shadow of the things that were to come . . . in Christ" (Colossians 2:17)? What shadows (celebrations, festivities, rhythms of life) point to the reality of Christ in our modern-day world?

_____

_____

_____

How do we experience shadows of the cycle of death and resurrection in the seasons of life around us?

_____

_____

_____

Pray: Close out your time today by praying to God about the reality of the true myth of Jesus Christ.

For Next Week: Read chapter five in *The Problem of God* and use the space below to write any insights or questions from your personal study that you want to discuss at the next group meeting.

Journal, Reflections, and Notes

_____

_____

_____

_____

_____

_____

_____

_____

_____

_____

_____

_____

_____

_____

_____

The Problem of
EVIL AND SUFFERING

*And we know that in all things God works for
the good of those who love him, who have been
called according to his purpose.*

—ROMANS 8:28

Welcome

One of the most common questions of humankind is this: *Why is there pain and suffering in the world?* Shortly after my parents divorced when I was eight years old, I developed a psychological disorder called Tourette syndrome, which later developed into obsessive-compulsive disorder. This meant that growing up, I would adopt a habit—a face twitch or random swearing at myself—for months at a time until another habit came along and replaced it. Because of the obsessive-compulsive disorder, I would superstitiously pound my hands together or smack myself in the face because if I didn't do these things, I was convinced something bad would happen to the people around me. If I didn't hit that post three times in the airport or tap my foot against the seat, the plane would go down, etc. It all sounds crazy now, but it was the reality for much of my life.

So, when I began to research and wrestle with the existence of God, I had lingering questions about suffering and evil that came from my own experience—my sickness and the early loss of my father. To anyone observing my early years of sickness, becoming a pastor would have seemed like the last job I'd ever get. Fast-forward twenty-plus years, and I conducted a funeral for a new friend named Andrew. A few months before I met Andrew, he was a healthy, active, competitive cyclist. He was also an amazing father with two beautiful kids and a loving, caring family. But a brain tumor left him blind and fading away. During Andrew's funeral, I looked at his children in the front row as they wept, and I felt the weight of their suffering. Standing there felt wrong, *evil*, disjointed from the way things should be. And I found myself asking the question we are tackling today: *How could God allow such evil and suffering in the world?*

Share 💬

To kick things off, briefly discuss one of the following:

- Name one reason why you think there is pain and suffering in the world.
  —or—
- If you could ask God one question, and you knew God would answer, what would it be?

Read 📖

Invite someone to read aloud the following passage as preparation for Mark's teaching. Listen for fresh insights as you hear the verses being read, and then briefly discuss the questions that follow.

ECCLESIASTES 3

There is a time for everything,
    and a season for every activity under the heavens:

a time to be born and a time to die,
a time to plant and a time to uproot,
a time to kill and a time to heal,
a time to tear down and a time to build,
a time to weep and a time to laugh,
a time to mourn and a time to dance,
a time to scatter stones and a time to gather them,
a time to embrace and a time to refrain from embracing,
a time to search and a time to give up,
a time to keep and a time to throw away,
a time to tear and a time to mend,
a time to be silent and a time to speak,
a time to love and a time to hate,
a time for war and a time for peace.

What do workers gain from their toil? I have seen the burden God has laid on the human race. He has made everything beautiful in its time. He has also set eternity in the human heart; yet no one can fathom what God has done from beginning to end. I know that there is nothing better for people than to be happy and to do good while they live. That each of them may eat and drink, and find satisfaction in all their toil— this is the gift of God. I know that everything God does will endure forever; nothing can be added to it and nothing taken from it. God does it so that people will fear him.

> Whatever is has already been,
>> and what will be has been before;
>> and God will call the past to account.
> And I saw something else under the sun:

> In the place of judgment—wickedness was there,
>> in the place of justice—wickedness was there.
> I said to myself,

> "God will bring into judgment
>> both the righteous and the wicked,
> for there will be a time for every activity,
>> a time to judge every deed."

I also said to myself, "As for humans, God tests them so that they may see that they are like the animals. Surely the fate of human beings is like that of the animals; the same fate awaits them both: As one dies, so dies the other. All have the same breath; humans have no advantage over animals. Everything is meaningless. All go to the same place; all come from dust, and to dust all return. Who knows if the human spirit rises upward and if the spirit of the animal goes down into the earth?"

So I saw that there is nothing better for a person than to enjoy their work, because that is their lot. For who can bring them to see what will happen after them?

What new insight do you notice in this passage?

_____

_____

_____

Consider as you listen to Mark's teaching, *how does suffering change us and our experience of God?*

_____

_____

_____

Watch ▶️

Play the video segment for session 5. As you watch, use the following outline to record any thoughts or concepts that stand out to you.

NOTES

Why is there pain and suffering in the world?

> One might well conclude that the world contains far too much misery for the pious idea for a good, loving and just God to be taken seriously. Any alleged creator of the Universe in which children seem to suffer and die hardly deserves our devotion. This is an effective, not strictly logical, position to hold, but an intelligible one with a certain sublime moral purity to it. I, myself, find it deeply compelling.
>
> —DAVID BENTLEY HART

——— The Problem of Evil and Suffering ———

> Is God willing to prevent evil but not able? Then he is impotent. Is he able, but not willing, then he is malevolent? Is he both able and willing? Why then is there evil?
>
> —DAVID HUME

Key Question: Is there a connection between evil and God's nonexistence?

THREE KEY ASSUMPTIONS OF THE PROBLEM OF EVIL AND SUFFERING

- Evil is real.
- If God exists, he is loving.
- Those two realities are not compatible.

ESSENTIAL UNDERSTANDINGS OF THE PROBLEM OF EVIL AND SUFFERING

1. This is a personal question.

> We feel it. It points us toward God's existence, not away from it.

2. This is a biblical question.

> Genesis 3: evil and suffering enter the world.

> I saw under the altar the souls of those who had been slain for the word of God and for the witness they had borne; they cried out with a loud voice, "O Sovereign Lord, holy and true, how long before thou wilt judge and avenge our blood on those who dwell upon the earth?"
>
> —REVELATION 6:9–10 RSV

> The Bible addresses evil and suffering head-on throughout Scripture.

3. This isn't just a Christian question, it's a universal question.

   New Age Philosophy:
   - Addresses the problem of evil and suffering with a combination of answers borrowed from its ancient roots in Eastern religion.
   - Pantheism: all is one, all is God, we are all reaching a higher state of enlightenment or illumination.
   - We are all part of the divine in some way.
   - Evil and suffering are "maya"—an illusion; it's not real.

   The Response of Biblical Truth:
   - Evil and suffering are real.
   - This is why God came to Earth in the form of Jesus to deal with evil and suffering.
      Hinduism:
   - Karma—what goes around comes around.
   - Reincarnation cycle

   Atheism:
   - Because evil and suffering exist, God does not exist.
   - Bad things happen because there is no such thing as a good, loving God.
   - The "rock" of atheism: the existence of suffering

But these assumptions are not true unless proven true.

Christians believe in five basic premises about God and evil: God exists. God is all-powerful. God is all-knowing. God is holy good. And evil exists. Atheists argue that these assertions can't all be true at the same time. The problem is the atheist must prove some proofs of why these things can't be true at the same time.

—ALVIN PLANTINGA

Atheistic attempts to prove assumptions:

A good thing, i.e. God, always eliminates evil as far as it can, and there are no limits to what an all-powerful thing can do. Ergo, God should eliminate all evil because he's all good and all-powerful.

—J. L. MACKIE

The Christian conclusion: Atheistic assumptions are too simplistic and do not match the Christian conception of God who is far more complex than our limited scope.

An all-powerful being could permit as much evil as he pleased, so long as for every evil state of affairs that he does permit, there is a greater good.

—ALVIN PLANTINGA

Help for a Skeptic on Suffering

Evil and suffering were actually powerful evidence for God's existence rather than against it.

—MARK CLARK

Categorical Evil: the skeptic's position assumes there is categorical evil.
Key Question: But where did these categories come from? Where did we get the idea of an inherent moral order of the universe?

When I was an atheist, my argument against God was that the universe seemed so cruel and unjust. But how had I got this idea of just and unjust? What was I comparing the universe with when I called it unjust? Of course, I could have just given up my idea of justice by saying that it was nothing but a private idea of my own. But if I did that, then my argument against God collapsed, too, for the argument depended on saying that the world was really unjust, not just simply that it did not happen to please my fancies.

—C. S. LEWIS

He has made everything beautiful in its time. He has also set eternity in the human heart; yet no one can fathom what God has done from beginning to end.

—ECCLESIASTES 3:11

We long for beauty and justice, for love and peace because we were created to live in a world without sin and death (Genesis 1 and 2).

——— Pointless Evil ———

If God exists, he would not allow pointless evil. And because there is so much unjustifiable, pointless evil in the world, the traditional God cannot exist.

—J. L. MACKIE

Key Question: How do we prove evil and suffering are pointless?
Perhaps the opposite is true: *Suffering has a purpose in the world.*
Suffering may actually lead to a measure of good.

The assumption that there is never a good reason for evil and suffering cannot be supported by philosophy, science, experience of life, or the testimony of history. It's not a defensible philosophical position.

—MARK CLARK

——— The Biblical Response to Suffering and Evil ———

All through the Scriptures, God uses suffering to make people who they are.

—MARK CLARK

Consider the suffering and evil experienced by people such as:

- Moses
- Abraham
- David
- Job
- Paul
- Jesus

The point: Be careful not to assume the meaning of suffering and evil. The meaning behind evil is not visible to the naked eye. But it's still real.

> So, why do we think of the purpose or the meaning of evil and suffering as a great dane vs. a noceum? Sometimes we just don't understand. That doesn't mean there isn't a purpose.
>
> —ALVIN PLANTINGA

The Struggle to Explain Evil and Suffering

We are too busy pursuing happiness in a material world.
Karmic Theology blames the victim for their fate.

> Christianity teaches that contra-fatalism suffering is overwhelming; contra-Buddhism, suffering is real; contra-karma, suffering is often unfair; but contra-secularism, suffering is meaningful.
>
> —TIMOTHY KELLER

The Cross of Christ

The cross of Christ is the moment where the love of God is revealed to the universe set against the contrast of human sin. This is why such suffering—the suffering of Jesus—was necessary.

God turns human evil into our redemption and salvation, as the greatest act of human evil—the killing of our Creator—is transformed into the supreme act of love.

—MARK CLARK

God preferred, on the whole, the global result of the drama of sin and salvation to a world without it. Evil was necessary for that drama and, thus, evil does have a place in the great scheme of things. Without it, there would be no such thing as endurance, bravery, sacrifice, and courage. In his wisdom, God said, "I want the greater good to happen."

—JOHN STACKHOUSE, JR.

God is not distant from our suffering. He suffers *with* us and *for* us.
Key Question: Why did God suffer for us?
Suffering as Revelation of God: Suffering reveals who God is, not just what he did.

And we know that in all things God works for the good of those who love him, who have been called according to his purpose.

—ROMANS 8:28

Our pain gives way to a greater glory.

I consider that the sufferings of this present time are not worth comparing with the glory that is to be revealed to us.

—ROMANS 8:18 ESV

Everything sad is going to come untrue.

—GANDALF IN *THE LORD OF THE RINGS*

The cross reveals what God has done about evil and suffering.
Key Question: Have you embraced the hope of Jesus that transcends your circumstances?
Christianity tells us that God suffered under evil so we don't have to labor anymore. When we understand this, it changes everything.

Group Discussion

Take a few minutes with your group members to discuss what you just watched and explore these concepts in Scripture. Then take time to pray together as a group. Use the space at the end of this session to keep track of prayer requests and group updates.

1. What stood out to you from Mark's teaching on the problem of evil and suffering?

    _____

    _____

    _____

2. Based on what we learned today, how can we reconcile the truth of the existence of a loving God with the existence of evil and suffering in the world?

    _____

    _____

    _____

3. As Mark said, how have you seen God use suffering to make people who they are today?

    _____

    _____

    _____

4. **Read Genesis 22:1–14.** After the infamous story of evil in the Garden of Eden, this seems to be the next experience of suffering we see in the Bible. How can you identify with the suffering of Abraham and Isaac leading up to the moment where the ram appears? Is there another specific example in the Bible of how you identify with the suffering of others?

    _____

    _____

    _____

5. Name some instances when God rescued you *before* or redeemed you *after* suffering. How has suffering shaped your experience of God?

_____

_____

_____

6. **Read Romans** 8:18–39. According to the apostle Paul, what happens when we place our hope and trust in Jesus in the midst of our suffering?

_____

_____

_____

Pray

Pray as a group before you close your time together. Thank God for the hope he brings through Jesus Christ amid the suffering and evil of the world. If you are still having a hard time wrapping your mind around the concepts of evil and suffering with God's existence, ask God for wisdom and understanding regarding your assumptions and experiences in life. May the truth of a loving God shine light in the darkness of the evil and suffering you experience in the world around you. Use this space to keep track of prayer requests and group updates.

_____

_____

_____

_____

_____

_____

_____

_____

_____

_____

_____

_____

Between-Sessions
PERSONAL STUDY

Weekly Reflection

Before you begin the between-sessions exercises, briefly review your video notes for session 5. In the space below, write down the *most significant point* you took away from this session.

_____

_____

_____

_____

Take some time to reflect on the material you covered during your group time by engaging in any or all of the following between-sessions exercises. As you read and experience the material, you may want to make a few notes in your guide. The primary goal of these between-sessions is for your own spiritual growth and personal reflection, and it is not a requirement for group participation. If you haven't done so already, read chapter five in *The Problem of God*.

Day 1: The Personal Side of Suffering
Read: *Psalm 6; Habakkuk 1–3*

Consider: In my work as a pastor, I visit families that have lost loved ones to disease, violence, and natural disasters. I get calls in the middle of the night that someone has committed suicide, adultery, or even murder. My own life is riddled with brokenness and pain at many levels. I lost an aunt to schizophrenic suicide. My childhood is filled with memories of an unstable home characterized by fighting, yelling, and slamming doors. My dad was an alcoholic who couldn't keep a job and didn't know what to do with two sons, so when I was eight, he abandoned us when he and my mom divorced. That's when I developed Tourette syndrome and obsessive-compulsive disorder which was debilitating at times, especially in high school. Then, at age fifteen, I got a call that my dad had died. There was no warning, no communication, just a phone call from a hospital administrator who delivered the news. And *I know you've felt this way before too.* You've watched the news or received a late-night phone call. You've felt sick and lost and abandoned. And it all feels so personal. *How could a loving God allow such things?* There is a good reason why we feel this way, why we ask this question. It's because suffering points us toward God's existence, not away from it. Just three chapters into the Bible, evil and suffering are already part of life on earth. The prophets and the psalmists go on to feel and write about this tension of suffering and evil in their personal lives and in the world around them. The Bible even tells us that people in heaven are asking the same question. The whole Bible is the story of how evil has affected us. It faces this question head-on and provides the most glorious answer: that God is with us in our suffering and provides a way out of evil.

Reflect: Take a few moments to reflect on your answers to these questions.

Why is David's soul in deep anguish (Psalm 6)? Describe a time when you felt like David.

_____

_____

_____

How can you identify with the story of Habakkuk?

_____

_____

_____

As you reflect on your own seasons of suffering, what encourages you about the way God responds to Habakkuk?

_____

_____

_____

Pray: Close out your time today by praying to God about the personal weight of suffering. May you see the grace and the glory of God in the midst of your own suffering.

Day 2: The Proof of Suffering
Read: *Job 1–2 and 40–42—the beginning and the end of the story of Job*

Consider: Years ago I was working at a church on the day a funeral was held for a sixteen-year-old boy. I had such angst about the service that I left the building, walked around town, and cried out to God. Why had this boy's life been cut so short? How could any good come from this pain? When I was done crying, I went to a coffee shop and sat there in a daze. A little while later, a man from our church came in and sat next to me. He had been at the funeral service, too. I shared my frustration and pain. He listened as I vented and then prayed for me. As he was getting up to leave, he told me a brief story of his own. He was headed down the wrong road when God completely transformed his life, and it all started at the funeral of a sixteen-year-old friend. It was there he heard the gospel for the first time and gave his life to Jesus. As I listened to his story, it was as though God peeled back the veil for a second to give me a glimpse of the bigger story: how good can come from suffering, even if we don't understand why or how it all works. All throughout Scripture, God uses suffering to make people who they are, to refine them. Moses, Abraham, David, Job, Paul, and Jesus are examples of lives in which the most awful evil and suffering are turned into a greater good. And the ultimate good came out of the suffering of Jesus—the salvation of humankind itself. Suffering is actually powerful evidence for God's existence, if we're willing to see it that way; if we're willing to allow it to reveal God to us, rather than disprove him or point us away from him.

Reflect: Take a few moments to reflect on your answers to these questions.

What stands out to you about the suffering of Job?

_____

_____

_____

How does God respond to Job's suffering near the end of this story?

_____

_____

_____

What does this tell you about God and his presence in the midst of our human struggles and your own suffering?

Pray: Close out your time today by praying to God about the proof of his existence in the middle of our suffering. May you learn to trust God's presence with you in the midst of your struggles.

Day 3: The Advantage of Disadvantage
Read: *John 3:1–21; John 5:16–23; Philippians 2:1–11*

Consider: We've already talked about the disadvantages I had as a youth—namely, Tourette syndrome and obsessive-compulsive disorder—and how they wreaked havoc on my life. In fact, I still struggle with some movement tics today. And I'm sure you can identify with having some kind of disadvantages in your own life, too. Author and entrepreneur Malcolm Gladwell coined a phenomenon, "the advantage of the disadvantage." In his book *David and Goliath*, Gladwell documents the lives of many successful leaders and entrepreneurs (we're talking billionaires around the world) who succeed because of their challenges and suffering, not in spite of them. On one hand, these leaders and entrepreneurs could be so smart and creative that nothing could stop them, *or* perhaps they succeeded *because* of their struggles. Perhaps their suffering caused them to learn something new that proved to be of enormous advantage. Suffering isn't just something that shapes us into better people, it's actually what allows us to identify with the very nature of God through Jesus. Suffering is a reflection of who God is, not just something he did. Through the humanity of Jesus, God identified and empathized with us, and he suffered with us and for us. And through this suffering, both our own suffering and the suffering of Jesus, we get to experience the greatest good: God's love. Though we may not understand all of the reasons why evil and suffering exist, it is possible that God allowed them to exist so that the greater good of his love could exist. In the face of evil and suffering, we have the opportunity to experience endurance, bravery, sacrifice, courage, and love—God's love. This is the advantage of disadvantage.

Reflect: Take a few moments to reflect on your answers to these questions.

What do these passages tell us about the relationship between God and Jesus?

_____

_____

_____

What do these passages reveal about our relationship with God, and as a result, our relationship with others?

_____

_____

_____

How has your suffering revealed the greatest good of God's love from God himself, and through the love of others?

_____

_____

_____

Pray: Close out your time today by praying to God about the way suffering and evil point to the existence and love of God. May you know this to be true in the world around you.

For Next Week: Read chapter six in *The Problem of God* and use the space below to write any insights or questions from your personal study that you want to discuss at the next group meeting.

Journal, Reflections, and Notes

_____

_____

_____

_____

_____

_____

_____

_____

_____

The Problem of
HELL

*"There will be weeping there, and gnashing of
teeth, when you see Abraham, Isaac and Jacob
and all the prophets in the kingdom of God,
but you yourselves thrown out."*

—LUKE 13:28

Welcome

As I wrestled through my own problems with God, namely, the reliability of the Bible, the legitimacy of miracles, and the dark history of the church, filled with judgment, violence, and hypocrisy, an even deeper struggle for me was the idea of hell. I wrestled with the doctrine of hell and how God could allow my father, who to my knowledge never became a Christian, to go to a place of everlasting torment. This didn't square with my understanding of justice, love, or Jesus. But this made me lean into and explore my doubts, rather than run away from them. And I wasn't alone on this journey. One of the greatest stumbling blocks for some people as they consider the claims of Christianity is the concept of hell. It's the deal-breaker for so many on the verge of placing their faith and trust in the Bible and in Jesus as Christ. The idea of an eternal place of punishment for those who don't trust Christ isn't just a frustration, many people find the idea appalling and repulsive. Hell presents multiple obstacles for people and raises several questions, like: How can an all-loving God judge people eternally for what they do in a finite amount of time? That's why it's important to explore all of the obstacles and what they have to say about this admittedly difficult doctrine. And when we do, I believe we will find a logical rationale for hell that may not have been clear before. Let's dive in.

Share 💬

To kick things off, briefly discuss one of the following:

- Name one reason why you think hell is a deal-breaker for so many people on the verge of placing their faith in Jesus.

    —*or*—

- If you could ask God one question about hell, what would it be?

Read 📖

Invite someone to read aloud the following passage as preparation for Mark's teaching. Listen for fresh insights as you hear the verses being read, and then briefly discuss the questions that follow.

LUKE 16:19–31

"There was a rich man who was dressed in purple and fine linen and lived in luxury every day. At his gate was laid a beggar named Lazarus, covered with sores and longing to eat what fell from the rich man's table. Even the dogs came and licked his sores.

"The time came when the beggar died and the angels carried him to Abraham's side. The rich man also died and was buried. In Hades, where he was in torment, he looked up and saw Abraham far away, with Lazarus by his side. So he called to him, 'Father Abraham, have pity on me and send Lazarus to dip the tip of his finger in water and cool my tongue, because I am in agony in this fire.'

"But Abraham replied, 'Son, remember that in your lifetime you received your good things, while Lazarus received bad things, but now he is comforted here and you are in agony. And besides all this, between us and you a great chasm has been set in place, so that those who want to go from here to you cannot, nor can anyone cross over from there to us.'

"He answered, 'Then I beg you, father, send Lazarus to my family, for I have five brothers. Let him warn them, so that they will not also come to this place of torment.'

"Abraham replied, 'They have Moses and the Prophets; let them listen to them.'

"'No, father Abraham,' he said, 'but if someone from the dead goes to them, they will repent.'

"He said to him, 'If they do not listen to Moses and the Prophets, they will not be convinced even if someone rises from the dead.'"

What new insight do you notice in this passage?

_____

_____

_____

Consider as you listen to Mark's teaching, *how does the reality of hell change God's posture toward us?*

_____

_____

_____

Watch ▶

Play the video segment for session 6. As you watch, use the following outline to record any thoughts or concepts that stand out to you.

NOTES

——— **The Concept of Hell** ———

Of all the doctrines of Christianity, hell is probably the most difficult to defend, the most burdensome to believe, and the first to be abandoned.

—PETER KREEFT

Hell: An eternal place of punishment for those who don't trust Christ in their life. *The reaction to hell*: It's more repulsion than doubt.

I do not myself feel that any person who's really profoundly humane can believe in everlasting punishment.

—BERTRAND RUSSELL

Hell presents multiple obstacles for people and raises a ton of questions.

——— The Explanation for Hell ———

There is no doctrine which I would more willingly remove from Christianity than this, if it lay in my power. But it has the full support of Scripture, and especially of our Lord's own words, and has always been held by Christendom, and it has the support of reason.

—C. S. LEWIS

The Fear-Factor: Fear as a primary motivator for people to move toward Christ. This does not translate into a long life of discipleship.

1. Hell is connected closely with the person and the teachings of Jesus.

There is one very serious defect to my mind in Christ's moral character, and that is that he believed in hell.

—BERTRAND RUSSELL, ATHEIST

Progressive Revelation: We get most of our understanding of hell from Jesus.

Thirteen percent of Jesus' teachings and half of his parables are about hell, judgment, punishment, and the wrath of God.

Examples:

"'Depart from me, you cursed, into the eternal fire prepared for the devil and his angels'. . . . And they will go away into eternal punishment, but the righteous into eternal life."

—MATTHEW 25:41, 46 RSV

"But the subjects of the kingdom will be thrown outside, into the darkness, where there will be weeping and gnashing of teeth."

—MATTHEW 8:12

"And if your hand causes you to sin, cut it off. It is better for you to enter life crippled than with two hands to go to hell, to the unquenchable fire . . . 'Where their worm does not die and the fire is not quenched.'"

—MARK 9:43, 48 ESV

If you want to get rid of hell, then you have to get rid of Jesus.

2. The major objections people have to the idea of hell:
   – Objection #1: Hell is repulsive.
      Key Question: Why are we repulsed by the idea of hell?
      Our cultural context informs our beliefs, including our beliefs about hell.
      Key Question: What alternative beliefs do we hold that we need to examine and question?

Hell is both eternal and conscious.

—MARK CLARK

There is a logic and justification for the traditional view of hell which makes much better sense of the biblical teaching and of rational thinking.

—MARK CLARK

Learn to distinguish the difference between liking something or not, and whether it's true or not.
   – Objection #2: Hell is unjust.
      It's the thinking that the punishment doesn't fit the crime.
      Universalism:

Until the nineteenth century, almost all Christian theologians taught the reality of eternal torment in hell. Here and there, outside the theological mainstream, were some who believed that the wicked would be finally annihilated, even fewer were advocates of universal salvation. Eternal punishment was firmly asserted in official creeds and confessions of the churches. It must have seemed as an indispensable part of the universal Christian belief as the doctrine of the Trinity and the incarnation.

—RICHARD BAUCKHAM

Key Questions: Is God just if he allows hell to exist or sends anyone there? Or how could God be just if there isn't a hell?

It takes the quiet of a suburban home for the birth of the thesis of God's refusal to judge. In a scorched land soaked in the blood of the innocent, it will invariably die. And as one watched it die, one will do well to reflect about many other pleasant captivities of the liberal mind.

—MIROSLAV VOLF, THEOLOGIAN

We are hardwired to cry out for justice in the face of injustice.
If God is truly just, then there is a hell.
The doctrine of hell and God's love are not mutually exclusive of one another.

People today tend to care only for the softer virtues [of God's character] like love and tenderness, while they've forgotten the hard virtues of holiness, righteousness, and justice.

—D. A. CARSON, NEW TESTAMENT SCHOLAR

– Objection #3: Hell is overkill.

To the degree to which a person experiences punishment is not typically based on how long it takes them to commit a crime. It's based on the seriousness of the crime.

—MARK CLARK

Punishment is based on the weight of the crime committed.
The moral offense of sin.
Our sin is an infinite offense against God. A cost must be paid for our sin.
Punishment must be applied according to reality.

Hell is God's great complement to the reality of human freedom and the dignity of human choice.

—G. K. CHESTERTON

Hell is not a place where people are consigned because they were pretty good people who didn't believe the right stuff. They are consigned there, first and foremost, because they defy their Maker and want to be at the center of the universe. Hell is not filled with people who have already repented, only God isn't gentle enough or good enough to let them out. It's filled with people who, for all eternity, still want to be the center of the universe. What is God to do? If he says it doesn't matter to him, then God is no longer a God to be admired. For him to act in any other way in the face of such blatant defiance would be to reduce God himself.

—D. A. CARSON

The experience of hell and heaven will not be the same for every person.

"Woe to you, Chora′zin! woe to you, Beth-sa′ida! for if the mighty works done in you had been done in Tyre and Sidon, they would have repented long ago in sackcloth and ashes. But I tell you, it shall be more tolerable on the day of judgment for Tyre and Sidon than for you. And you, Caper′na-um, will you be exalted to heaven? You shall be brought down to Hades. For if the mighty works done in you had been done in Sodom, it would have remained until this day. But I tell you that it shall be more tolerable on the day of judgment for the land of Sodom than for you."

—MATTHEW 11:21–24 RSV

Other passages regarding final judgment and punishment:
John 5
Matthew 25
Revelation 20
Romans 2

The reason these judgment passages focus so clearly on the whole context of a person's life and not just what they believe about some doctrines is because our life and what we do with it will directly equal the measure of judgment or glory we experience for all eternity.

—MARK CLARK

Proportional judgment and blessing.

– Objection #4: Hell is a torture chamber.

I couldn't hold someone's hand to a fire for a moment. How could a loving God, just because you don't obey him and do what he wants, torture you forever, not allowing you to die but to continue in that pain for eternity? There is no criminal who would do this.

—CHARLES TEMPLETON

Apocalyptic Imagery: Jesus uses apocalyptic imagery to make a point when he said there will be fire, darkness, weeping, and gnashing of teeth (Matthew 7; Mark 9).

For example: Fire is a common literary image for judgment.

The lake of fire in which Satan and his angels are thrown is not literal since Satan along with his angels is a spiritual being. The fire is a punishment that's not physical but spiritual in nature.

—GREG BEALE, NEW TESTAMENT SCHOLAR

. . . for our "God is a consuming fire."

—HEBREWS 12:29

These images point to something true and real.

All descriptions and depictions of heaven and hell in the Bible are symbolic and metaphorical. Each metaphor suggests one aspect of the experience of hell. For example, fire tells us of the disintegration, while darkness tells us of the isolation. Having said that, this does not at all imply that heaven and hell are metaphors. They are very much realities. But all language about them is elusive, metaphorical, and partial.

—TIMOTHY KELLER

The use of symbols in the Bible:

The reality behind the symbol is greater than the symbol itself.

—MARK CLARK

——— What Hell Is in Reality ———

According to the teachings of Jesus, hell is an awful, hopeless, and lonely existence.
Hell is the opposite of pleasure, joy, grace, and love.
Hell is a warning.

> It is not about your wife or your son, nor about Nero or Judas Iscariot. It is about you
> and me.
>
> —C. S. LEWIS

Key Question: Why is hell the way it is?

> In one sense, hell can be understood as the outworking of our choice to experience
> total autonomy from God. We're allowed to be our own god; we're allowed to sustain
> and provide for ourselves. The problem is, that's impossible.
>
> —MARK CLARK

Luke 16: Hell is a place without water.
Hell is the place where the common graces and blessings of God no longer exist.
Matthew 25: Hell was prepared as a place for the devil and his angels, but when people
choose to follow the devil in rebellion, they suffer the same consequences.
The choice we have every day: *To receive the salvation of God or reject it.*
Key Question: Whose will is sovereign in your life—God's will or yours?

> There are only two kinds of people: those who say, "Thy will be done" to God, and
> those to whom God says in the end, "Thy will be done." All those who are in hell
> choose it. No soul that seriously and constantly desires joy will ever miss it. I believe
> that the damned are successful rebels until the end. They enjoy the horrible freedom
> which they have demanded.
>
> —C. S. LEWIS

Key Question: What are we demanding?
The Bible tells us that hell is real and rational.

Group Discussion

Take a few minutes with your group members to discuss what you just watched and explore these concepts in Scripture. Then take time to pray together as a group. Use the space at the end of this session to keep track of prayer requests and group updates.

1. What stood out to you from Mark's teaching on the problem of hell?

2. How does the rational reality of hell change our posture toward God?

3. **Read Matthew 25:31–46.** According to this passage, who deserves eternal punishment, and why?

4. **Read Mark 9:42–50.** What kind of metaphorical language and apocalyptic imagery is used in this passage? Why do you think Jesus speaks in this way to his audience?

5. How would you answer Mark's final question: Whose will is sovereign in your life—God's or your own? How does understanding the reality of hell motivate you to take specific steps this week to begin to let God reign in your life?

Pray

Pray as a group before you close your time together. Thank God for the graces and blessings of a life in connection and communion with God. If you are still having a hard time wrapping your mind around the reality and rationale of hell, ask God for wisdom and understanding regarding the existence of hell. May God's love and the warning of hell, a place without the love of God, draw you to choose God for eternity. Use this space to keep track of prayer requests and group updates.

SESSION 6

Between-Sessions
PERSONAL STUDY

Weekly Reflection

Before you begin the between-sessions exercises, briefly review your video notes for session 6. In the space below, write down the *most significant point* you took away from this session.

   Take some time to reflect on the material you covered during your group time by engaging in any or all of the following between-sessions exercises. As you read and experience the material, you may want to make a few notes in your guide. The primary goal of these between-sessions activities is for your own spiritual growth and personal reflection, and it is not a requirement for group participation. If you haven't done so already, read chapter six in *The Problem of God.*

Day 1: Fear as Motivation for Hell
Read: *Proverbs 9:1–12; Philippians 2:12–18*

   Consider: I was nine years old when I first encountered the idea of hell. And I'm guessing the same might be true for you, too, if you grew up in church and went to Christian summer camp. And if you didn't, then let me set the stage for you. At the start of the week of camp, the nightly large-group messages were light, focused on a personal relationship with God, and frankly, quite fun.
   But as the week progressed, the messages got more and more serious—and dark. Then came

the final message on Friday night—the last message of the week before we left for home on Saturday morning. I later learned that Friday night was referred to as the "turn-or-burn" night. My camp friends and I gathered around a fire pit in the middle of the campground to sing songs and play games before heading to bed. The speaker stood up, threw some gas on the campfire, and as the flames shot up into the air, he said, "Do you want that to be you?" (Um, . . . no.) "Then believe in Jesus!" To which we all said yes, of course. The conversation afterward centered on the fear of hell rather than the love of Jesus. Which makes sense because who *wants* to go to hell? The presentation that night was driven by the idea that *fear* would motivate people toward long-lasting faith in Christ. Which, in the end, doesn't really work.

Don't get me wrong, fear can motivate us. But fear as the primary and exclusive reason to trust in Christ rarely translates into a life of discipleship. Mishandling the doctrine of hell and the reality of God's judgment can damage a person's faith. And it's helpful to be aware of how this danger has impacted your own faith journey, as well as those around you.

Reflect: Take a few moments to reflect on your answers to these questions.

How do these passages define fear?

_____

_____

_____

What is the difference between fear as reverent respect for God and his forgiveness of our sin vs. the campfire fear of hell?

_____

_____

_____

How does the mishandling of fear as the motivation for not going to hell resonate with your own faith story? And how does it inform the way you talk to others about the reality of hell?

_____

_____

_____

Pray: Close out your time today by praying to God about how to engage in conversation about the reality of hell without using fear as motivation. May you know the peace of God amidst the presentation of the salvation message.

Day 2: Hell according to Jesus
Read: *Matthew 7:13–20; Matthew 8:5–13; Mark 9:42–49*

Consider: It's likely that most people think our understanding of hell comes from the Old Testament, but the greatest insight comes from the words of Jesus. A solid understanding of hell is closely connected to the person of Jesus and his teaching. So, if you want to get rid of hell, then you have to get rid of Jesus. He's the one who teaches about the existence and the nature of hell most directly and explicitly.

But here's the irony: people often say they don't like the Old Testament God who seems angry and full of wrath, always punishing people; they much prefer the New Testament because of Jesus, who seems to be more about love, grace, and full of teaching about helpful spiritual ideas. But what they don't realize is half of Jesus' parables and 13 percent of his teachings are about hell, judgment, punishment, and the wrath of God. If we are willing to acknowledge the *love of God* through Jesus in the New Testament, then we also have to acknowledge that the *wrath of God* gets ratcheted up in the New Testament, too. There is no escaping the fact that hell is a Jesus-driven teaching central to the New Testament, just as much as the love and the grace of God.

Reflect: Take a few moments to reflect on your answers to these questions.

What stands out to you about the way Jesus talks about hell?

What are the warnings and instructions Jesus gives to his followers?

How does the reality of Jesus' teachings about hell influence the way you think and talk about hell?

_____

_____

_____

Pray: Close out your time today by praying to God as you accept the reality of hell through the teachings of Jesus. May you embrace the idea of hell acknowledged in the teachings of Jesus.

Day 3: More Than Just a Symbol
Read: *Matthew 13:24–43; Luke 13:22–28; Revelation 20*

Consider: The language about hell throughout the New Testament is suggestive rather than direct, symbolic, and metaphorical. But make no mistake, the depictions are very much reality. It's as if you're walking through a mall and the custodian was mopping the floor, you would most likely see a bright yellow sign nearby with a picture of a man mid-slip and falling. This is the standard "caution, slippery when wet" sign. You might look at that sign and think, "Whoa, that experience looks harsh!" But if you personally hit a wet patch on the floor and fell, smacking your head, you would likely agree that while the picture looked awful, the experience was far worse. This is how this all works.

Most of the pictures we find in the Bible are pictures of a reality not *less* but more *real* than the picture itself. Symbols are powerful things pointing us toward a deeper reality than what the image, or imagination, can capture. The reality behind the symbol is greater than the symbol itself. Hell is real and scary. But in that reality, there is a seriousness that can give way to security if we trust the one who took hell on himself for us. Jesus, driven by love and desire for all to have eternal life and for no one to perish, saved us from hell to the glorious and wonderful greater good: the love of God. The pictures of hell are intended to save us from the consequences of rejecting God and instead send us toward the loving arms of Jesus as God.

Reflect: Take a few moments to reflect on your answers to these questions.

What modern-day symbolism and imagery do we use daily to communicate a reality that's more "real" in person? (hint: consider the symbols and signs you see every day around you)

_____

_____

_____

What kind of symbolism and imagery is used to describe hell in these passages?

_____

_____

_____

According to these passages, what can you tell about the way the first-century audience of the New Testament writers responds to the descriptions of hell? What makes these descriptions so repulsive to most people today?

_____

_____

_____

Pray: Close out your time today by praying to God about how the symbolism and metaphors used by Jesus point to a deeper reality of the consequences of hell for those who reject God's gift of salvation. May you see the glorious and wonderful greater good in God's ways.

For Next Week: Read chapter seven in *The Problem of God* and use the space below to write any insights or questions from your personal study that you want to discuss at the next group meeting.

Journal, Reflections, and Notes

_____

_____

_____

_____

_____

_____

_____

_____

_____

_____

_____

_____

_____

The Problem of
SEX

Every good and perfect gift is from above.

—JAMES 1:17

Welcome

When I became a Christian at seventeen, I studied the Bible deeply, and I encountered ideas that were very counterintuitive to my views at the time. One was the doctrine of hell, considering that just two years earlier I had buried my father. As far as I knew, my dad never trusted Jesus as his savior in his forty-seven years on earth. And twenty years later, when I showed up to bury my grandfather at age ninety-eight, I'm pretty certain he died with no faith in Jesus either. But the objections I had to the doctrine of hell were *cultural* ones—born out of sensibilities and ideals I held because I was a twenty-first-century, white, middle-class, educated Westerner with all the accompanying perks I am not even aware of at times. When I forced myself to see through my objections in order to understand the Bible's teaching in context, I realized there is logic and justification for hell just as there is for the way Jesus talks about human sexuality.

It's important to understand that many of our objections to the Christian view of human sexuality are the by-product of the ideals of the Western world—the "priorities of the autonomous self." These Western ideals are reflected in the notion that any limit on our behavior is a violation of our basic human rights as individuals. We believe the ultimate expression of our freedom and our autonomy is to use our bodies in whatever way we want, as long as we are content. In other words, we are good capitalists when it comes to human sexuality. But the biblical perspective on sex is robust and stands contrary to popular alternative views: *sex is bad, sex is god,* and *sex is appetite.* Let's take a closer look.

Share 💬

To kick things off, briefly discuss one of the following:

- Name one reason why you think sex gets a bad rap in our culture today.

  —*or*—

- Who had "the talk" with you about human sexuality? Briefly share one or two things you remember about that experience.

Read 📖

Invite someone to read aloud the following passage as preparation for Mark's teaching. Listen for fresh insights as you hear the verses being read, and then briefly discuss the questions that follow.

PROVERBS 5

My son, pay attention to my wisdom,
  turn your ear to my words of insight,
that you may maintain discretion
  and your lips may preserve knowledge.
For the lips of the adulterous woman drip honey,
  and her speech is smoother than oil;
but in the end she is bitter as gall,
  sharp as a double-edged sword.
Her feet go down to death;
  her steps lead straight to the grave.
She gives no thought to the way of life;
  her paths wander aimlessly, but she does not know it.

Now then, my sons, listen to me;
  do not turn aside from what I say.
Keep to a path far from her,
  do not go near the door of her house,

lest you lose your honor to others
    and your dignity to one who is cruel,
lest strangers feast on your wealth
    and your toil enrich the house of another.
At the end of your life you will groan,
    when your flesh and body are spent.
You will say, "How I hated discipline!
    How my heart spurned correction!
I would not obey my teachers
    or turn my ear to my instructors.
And I was soon in serious trouble
    in the assembly of God's people."

Drink water from your own cistern,
    running water from your own well.
Should your springs overflow in the streets,
    your streams of water in the public squares?
Let them be yours alone,
    never to be shared with strangers.
May your fountain be blessed,
    and may you rejoice in the wife of your youth.
A loving doe, a graceful deer—
    may her breasts satisfy you always,
    may you ever be intoxicated with her love.
Why, my son, be intoxicated with another man's wife?
    Why embrace the bosom of a wayward woman?

For your ways are in full view of the LORD,
    and he examines all your paths.
The evil deeds of the wicked ensnare them;
    the cords of their sins hold them fast.
For lack of discipline they will die,
    led astray by their own great folly.

What new insight do you notice in this passage?

_____

_____

_____

Consider as you listen to Mark's teaching, *why is discipline such an important aspect of healthy sexuality from a Christian perspective?*

_____

_____

_____

Watch ▶

Play the video segment for session 7. As you watch, use the following outline to record any thoughts or concepts that stand out to you.

NOTES

──── Human Sexuality ────

The worst feature of the Christian religion is its attitude towards sex. Christianity's teaching about sex has been deemed oppressive, antiquated. In other words, if we wish to have a constructive discussion about sex as a culture, if we wish to be truly free as individuals, then the Christian perspective has no place in the discussion because it's oppressive.

—BERTRAND RUSSELL

──── A Christian Perspective ────

Key Question: Why do people have a major problem with Christianity's teaching on sexuality?
The Western world prioritizes the autonomy of the self.

We have a society built around the priority of the autonomous self. From the Enlightenment to today, the highest good in our culture has been freely choosing autonomous individuals, deciding out of rational self-interest to construct a progressive society.

—DARRELL L. GUDER

Limits on our behavior are seen and felt like a violation.

The ultimate expression of freedom and our autonomy: To use our bodies in whatever way we choose.

Sex is seen as one of the great joys in our lives, but God is seen as the one who restricts us and limits us from these joys.

——— The Truth: Sex Is God's Idea ———

Sex is more than a personal, autonomous experience.

——— How the Christian Perspective Counters the Two Popular Views Today ———

1. First Popular View: *Sex Is Bad*

   The Christian View: God created sex to be a good thing.

   > God made the wild animals according to their kinds, the livestock according to their kinds, and all the creatures that move along the ground according to their kinds. And God saw that it was good.
   >
   > —GENESIS 1:25

   > God saw all that he had made, and it was very good. And there was evening, and there was morning—the sixth day.
   >
   > —GENESIS 1:31

   Paul dealt with sexual perversions in the church at Corinth, where bad theology that sex is a bad thing had also infiltrated the church.

   > Now for the matters you wrote about: "It is good for a man not to have sexual relations with a woman." But since sexual immorality is occurring, each man should have sexual relations with his own wife, and each woman with her own husband. The husband should fulfill his marital duty to his wife, and likewise the wife to her husband.
   >
   > —1 CORINTHIANS 7:1–3

According to Paul, the best way to combat a bad theology about sex is to have a healthy, robust sex life, if you're married.

> Do not deprive each other except perhaps by mutual consent and for a time, so that you may devote yourselves to prayer. Then come together again so that Satan will not tempt you because of your lack of self-control.
>
> —1 CORINTHIANS 7:5

Skeptics argue that the Bible restricts sex, except for pro-creation.
According to Paul's teaching, we see that frequency is important.
Sex Life Statistics:

- Couples under the age of 24 have sex an average of 132 times per year (every 2–3 days)
- Married couples under the age of 30 have sex about 2–3 times per week
- Married couples, in general, have sex with their spouse about 58 times per year, or a little more than once a week, on average
- 15 percent of married couples have not had sex with their spouse in the last six months to one year

> The point of Paul's exhortation is to make sure married couples are giving one another their conjugal rights to protect them from temptations.
>
> —MARK CLARK

A healthy goal:

> Twice a week seems to be enough to stave off the tempter.
>
> —MARTIN LUTHER

A healthy sex life is always two-sided—both the husband and the wife must contribute to the goal.

Contrary to the romanticism of our culture, we don't always have to wait for the "right mood" to have sex.

The wife does not have authority over her own body but yields it to her husband. In the same way, the husband does not have authority over his own body but yields it to his wife.

—1 CORINTHIANS 7:4

A husband is called to minister to his wife's spirit, which is one of her deepest needs, even though he may not feel like it at a given moment.

—EMERSON EGGERICHS (BASED ON EPHESIANS 5:33)

Serving our spouse's needs should be the priority over serving our own needs. Sexual pleasure for a woman is tied closely to her emotional life . . . the female brain. This is why context matters for women.

Female sexual turn-on begins, ironically, with a brain turn-off. The impulses can rush to the pleasure centers only if the amygdala, the fear and anxiety center of the brain, has been deactivated. Any worry about work, the kids, schedules, dinner can interrupt the march towards pleasure.

—DR. LOUANN BRIZENDINE

The difference between men and women.

40% of married people have sex twice a week compared to 20% of single and cohabitating men and women. . . . Over 40% of married women said their sex life was emotionally and physically satisfying, compared to 30% of single women. Of all sexually active people, the most physically pleased and sexually satisfied were married couples.

—LINDA WAITE AND MAGGIE GALLAGHER

Good sex takes hard work and time to get it right.

Maximum pleasure takes the amazing and exclusive relationship of marriage between a man and a woman.

—MARK CLARK

More Stats:

10% of women never experience orgasm

More than 50% of women have trouble getting one

The main reason for this: experiencing an orgasm is actually a learned skill.

The Bible's heart toward sexuality is that sex contributes to our flourishing for the glory of God.

> May your fountain be blessed,
>> and may you rejoice in the wife of your youth.
> A loving doe, a graceful deer—
>> may her breasts satisfy you always,
>> may you ever be intoxicated with her love.
>> —PROVERBS 5:18–19

> . . . your breasts like clusters of fruit.
> I said, "I will climb the palm tree;
>> I will take hold of its fruit."
>> —SONG OF SONGS 7:7–8S

> I have come into my garden, my sister, my bride;
>> I have gathered my myrrh with my spice.
> I have eaten my honeycomb and my honey;
>> I have drunk my wine and my milk.
>> —SONG OF SONGS 5:1A

Song of Songs is full of sexual metaphors and erotic poetry.

> Eat, friends, and drink;
>> drink your fill of love.
>> —SONG OF SONGS 5:1B

God rejoices in our sexual pleasure in a committed marriage relationship.

The role of the woman throughout the Song of Solomon is truly astounding, especially in light of its ancient origins. It is the woman, not the man, who is the dominant voice throughout the poems that make up the Song. She's the one who seeks, pursues, initiates. She boldly exclaims her physical attraction. "His abdomen is like a polished ivory tusk, decorated with sapphires." Most English translations hesitate in this verse. The Hebrew is quite erotic. And most translators cannot bring themselves to the obvious meaning. This is a prelude to their lovemaking. There is no shy, shame, mechanical movement under the sheets, rather the two stand before each other aroused, feeling no shame, but only joy in each other's sexuality.

—TREMPER LONGMAN III, OLD TESTAMENT SCHOLAR

To equate sex with Satan, evil, or sin is to miss one of the greatest expressions of God's love toward humankind.

2. Second Popular View: *Sex Is God*

Sexual liberation is the only method to finding inner peace, and security, and beauty. Remove the constraints and prohibitions which now hinder the release of inner energies and most of the larger evils of society will perish. Through sex, mankind will attain the great spiritual illumination which will transform the world and light up the only path to an earthly paradise.

—MARGARET SANGER

What is at stake with this kind of thinking is godliness and our personal and cultural flourishing.

The church can be present for people: We love and we listen after others have moved on.

Christianity teaches that sex is holistic.

Many of the best things in life actually require discipline, restriction, and focus so we can flourish. The greater "yes" is only possible when we say "no" to other things in life in a million ways.

—MARK CLARK

The concern of the passage as a whole is to call the Corinthians to act as a community and to stop seeing themselves as participants in the "normal" social and economical structures in their city; to imagine themselves, instead, as members of the people of God, acting corporately in a way that will prefigure and proclaim the kingdom of God. Paul is seeking to re-socialize them into a new way of doing business, a new community consciousness.

—RICHARD B. HAYS

The Christian version of sexuality is countercultural, but it is life-giving.
It answers the question of why sex exists.
It helps us maximize our pleasure while enjoying sex as a gift from God.

———— Jesus and Marriage ————

Jesus gives few reasons to divorce and mentions adultery (Matthew 19).
Marriage is a pointer to an eternal reality; it's not the end goal or the greatest pleasure.
Marriage is for the present age, not forever.

"At the resurrection people will neither marry nor be given in marriage; they will be like the angels in heaven."

—MATTHEW 22:30

Marriage is momentary, a brief blessing; a great one but not an ultimate one; a precious one, but not a permanent one. This eternal perspective explains why Jesus can be so radical. Never to have married is not a tragedy, otherwise, Jesus' life is a tragedy. Tragedy is craving the perfect marriage so much that we make a god out of being married. Jesus' standards are high because marriage does not and should not meet all our needs. It should not be an idol. It should not take the place of Jesus himself. Marriage is but for a moment, Jesus is for eternity. How we live in our marriages, in our singleness will show if Jesus is our supreme treasure.

—JOHN PIPER

Christians are to be sexually subversive by showing that Jesus, not sex, is our ultimate satisfaction.

——— Pleasure: A Gift from God ———

All pleasure is a grace given to us by God.

> Every good and perfect gift is from above . . .
>
> —JAMES 1:17

> It's a pointer to the eternal delight of the soul that we will have in heaven alone. It points to the deep infinitely fulfilling and final union we will have with Christ. It's the most ecstatic breath-taking scarcely to be imagined look at the glory that is our future.
>
> —TIMOTHY AND KATHY KELLER

Sex should draw us closer to God, instead of keeping us away from him.

God created sexuality.

Key Question: Don't you want to know the One who can give that kind of pleasure?

Group Discussion

Take a few minutes with your group members to discuss what you just watched and explore these concepts in Scripture. Then take time to pray together as a group. Use the space at the end of this session to keep track of prayer requests and group updates.

1. What stood out to you from Mark's teaching on the problem of sex?

    _____

    _____

    _____

2. If you are single, married, or divorced, how does the Christian teaching of sex relate to you? It's important to hear various points of view so be sure to include all voices represented in your group as you answer this question.

    _____

    _____

3. **Read Song of Songs 7.** How does the language and imagery in this passage illuminate a view of healthy sexuality?

4. **Read 1 Corinthians 7:1–16 and 25–40, and Ephesians 5:25–33.** Why do you think the apostle Paul, a single guy, spends so much time talking about marriage in his New Testament letters? What stands out to you in this passage in light of Mark's teaching today?

5. Mark says the Christian view of sexuality is countercultural and at the same time, life-giving. In general, how can this be true? Without sharing intimate details, how has this been true for you?

6. How does this teaching change the way you will respond when you hear others say, "Sex is bad" or, "Sex is god"?

Pray

Pray as a group before you close your time together. Thank God for the gift of pleasure in human sexuality. If you are single and struggling with this view, ask God to make his presence known to you. No matter where you are in your intimate relationships, may you know that these relationships are not the end-all but the pointer to a greater sense of flourishing in the goodness of God. Use this space to keep track of prayer requests and group updates.

Between-Sessions
PERSONAL STUDY

Weekly Reflection

Before you begin the between-sessions exercises, briefly review your video notes for session 7. In the space below, write down the *most significant point* you took away from this session.

_____

_____

_____

_____

   Take some time to reflect on the material you covered during your group time by engaging in any or all of the following between-sessions exercises. As you read and experience the material, you may want to make a few notes in your guide. The primary goal of these between-sessions activities is for your own spiritual growth and personal reflection, and it is not a requirement for group participation. If you haven't done so already, read chapter seven in *The Problem of God*.

> **Day 1:** The "Sex Is Bad" Myth
> **Read:** *Genesis 1:25–31; Deuteronomy 24:5; Proverbs 5:15–21; 1 Corinthians 7:1–7*
> *(and if you have extra time, enjoy reading Song of Songs 1–7)*

   Consider: In my late teens I started reading the Bible for myself and discovered something profound: My ideas about Christianity were actually not biblical, *at all*. Thanks to the influence of Western culture, I had marginalized views of the Christian attitude toward sex that were almost the *opposite* of what I found to be true. Since my early days of Christian summer camp, I thought God was against sex because everything I had heard about it from church leaders was negative. And as I remember one preacher putting it, "Sex is dirty, nasty, vile, and wrong . . . so save it for the one you love!" And then I found out that some churches prayed to Mary because she was a *virgin*, and this was the exact opposite of what I wanted to be! All of this was enough for me to keep Christianity at arm's length from my teenage mind and my hormone-driven body. I preferred to stuff my head full of images from music videos rather than accept the Christian view on sex. No thank you.

But when I started reading my Bible and challenging my assumptions, I learned that God was the one who *created* sex, and that he celebrated and encouraged it among human beings. So, rather than believe the Christian misinterpretations which have popped up throughout history and caused a lot of damage, the true biblical picture should be our starting point for understanding a Christian view of sex. When we do this, we see that sex is not *bad* or something to be avoided. It is beautiful, God-given, and meant to be *enjoyed* in the context of marriage.

Reflect: Take a few moments to reflect on your answers to these questions.

How have you experienced the "sex is bad" myth?

_____

_____

_____

What do these passages tell us about the biblical view of sex? What kinds of symbolism and metaphors are used to describe sex?

_____

_____

_____

How does this perspective differ from what you thought or were taught about a Christian view of sex? And how does this perspective differ from a secular perspective on sex?

_____

_____

_____

Pray: Close out your time today by praying to God about the actual biblical perspective of sex. May you know that God created sex for our pleasure and enjoyment within a committed marital relationship.

Day 2: The "Sex Is God" Myth
Read: *Matthew 22:30; Ephesians 5*

Consider: Throughout history, people have oriented their lives around the pursuit of sexual pleasure. Maybe you know this to be true based on your own experience of living and thinking this way. This kind of "sex-is-god" thinking, where sex is the *ultimate good*, was as normal in the first century as it is today. In fact, the Bible was written to people living in a culture of extreme sexual perversion: premarital sex, sexual slavery, temple prostitution, orgies, homosexuality, and various forms of promiscuity.

While we still live in a sex-driven culture, the form and accessibility have evolved over time. Many people think of sex as their salvation—that it will set them free, bringing peace on earth and goodwill toward men. With this view, sex becomes the central component of our identity as human beings, and thus freely satisfying our sexual appetites in whatever way we want is essential to our emotional health and wellbeing. This view believes that sex is the one and only way to experience earthly paradise. But this modern form of sexual liberation where sex is all about self-realization and personal, private behavior is far more threatening to the well-being of humanity than we realize because it isolates sexuality from the whole picture of what it means to be human.

We are more intimately connected than we realize. This is why the biblical story is so important. God gives sex as a gift and stitches sexual intimacy into history as the greatest and most powerful nonverbal signal of unity, love, covenant, and commitment—even a picture of the gospel message itself. Two become one in the act of sex. Our separate souls and personhoods create an entity and unity that did not exist before the act took place. The analogy of marriage in the Bible teaches us that while sex is amazing, it is not god, and there is a greater joy that will one day retire it.

Reflect: Take a few moments to reflect on your answers to these questions.

What stands out to you about the way Jesus mentions marriage in Matthew 22?

What changes for you, if anything, when you read Ephesians 5 in its entire context instead of just the marriage verses (21–33)? What difference does it make to see Paul start with "Follow God's example . . . and walk in the way of love" (verses 1 and 2)?

_____

_____

_____

How is the biblical perspective of sex "walking in the way of love" compared to our cultural view of sex-as-god?

_____

_____

_____

Pray: Close out your time today by praying to God about the view of sex that points to the ultimate and eternal treasure of a relationship with God. May you see the value in waiting for sex within the commitment of marriage as you honor your relationship with God.

> **Day 3:** The "Sex Is Appetite" Myth
> **Read:** *1 Corinthians 6:13–20; James 1:1–18*

Consider: When we get hungry, we eat whatever is around. When we get thirsty, we drink whatever we can find. When we are aroused, some of us think we can satisfy our needs by having sex with whomever is around—that we have a *natural appetite* for sex. But this idea is not real sex; it's simply animal-kingdom style mating. This perspective, as popular in the first century as it is today, attaches no moral value to the behavior of sex. A naturalistic approach that sanctions our biological appetites removes all moral culpability from our sexual choices.

That's why the apostle Paul critiques this view in a powerful and fascinating way. He insists that sex is an act that engages and expresses the whole personality. In other words, we never just have sex with a body; we have sex with a unique human *being* in a way that involves self-disclosure and self-commitment. Sex is more than just an appetite; it's a physical, emotional, and spiritual experience. When all that matters is our animal appetite, sex becomes a selfish endeavor.

But what the Bible teaches is something quite different and quite radical: Sex is *other-centered*, a selfless expression where a person joins his or her soul to another person's soul. The Bible says to have sex with someone is to *know* each other in every way. God created sex so that we would experience maximum pleasure, security, unity, and joy in a covenant (marriage) relationship. This is God's plan for human flourishing, and to do anything else will always fall short. And in this way, sex should draw us all closer to God as it points to the intimacy of our covenantal relationship with him.

Reflect: Take a few moments to reflect on your answers to these questions.

How do we honor God with our sexuality?

_____

_____

_____

What does Paul mean when he says our bodies were "meant . . . for the Lord and the Lord for the body" (1 Corinthians 6:13)?

_____

_____

_____

What makes sex one of the "good and perfect" gifts "from above" (James 1:17)?

_____

_____

_____

Pray: Close out your time today by praying to God about the purpose of our sexual desires as a way for human flourishing within the context of marriage. May we see how our desires point to eternity with God.

For Next Week: Read chapter eight in *The Problem of God* and use the space below to write any insights or questions from your personal study that you want to discuss at the next group meeting.

Journal, Reflections, and Notes

The Problem of
HYPOCRISY

"For no good tree bears bad fruit, nor again does a bad tree bear good fruit."

—LUKE 6:43 ESV

Welcome

If you believe the church is full of hypocrites, I agree with you. But thanks be to God that our faith is not about us; rather it's about him. In fact, no one puts a higher moral demand on people than Jesus. To live as new creations in the world, fighting injustice and absorbing violence at every turn, was the vision Jesus laid down for his people. The Bible calls us to judge the truth of Christianity by the life of Jesus, not by the lives of those attempting to follow him, because in him and him alone will you find someone worthy of trust and imitation. That's why it doesn't shake me when I meet with Christians in my sphere of influence who are "messy"—Christians who are skeptical, who have made poor choices to look at porn, do drugs, lie, cheat and steal, and lead immoral lives.

Let's face it, we've all made hypocritical choices at some point in our lives that go against the gospel message of Jesus. And yet we're quick to "throw the baby out with the bathwater" and reject Christianity based on the unjust actions of one bad apple who claims to be a Christian. We can continue rejecting Christianity in this way, or we can recognize that when the kingdom of God comes into a person's life, it causes upheaval, and sin gets exposed. At times, the collective sin of entire generations of people is reflected in history, and at times, the church must simply admit it has failed to live out the peaceful, loving commands of Jesus.

But we must remember that the church consists of people who have come to a place where they are trusting Jesus to save them, not because they are perfect already, but because they are not. True Christianity does not tear down or destroy enemies; it gives them a glass of water and washes their feet. This is the teaching of Jesus that gets lost in the hypocrisy of sin throughout the ages. Let's take a deeper look at the problem of hypocrisy.

Share 💬

To kick things off, briefly discuss one of the following:

- Name one or two ways you've seen injustices committed and excused in the name of Christianity.

   —or—
- What comes to mind when you hear the criticism of Christian hypocrisy?

Read 📖

Invite someone to read aloud the following passage as preparation for Mark's teaching. Listen for fresh insights as you hear the verses being read, and then briefly discuss the questions that follow.

JEREMIAH 23:1–17

"Woe to the shepherds who are destroying and scattering the sheep of my pasture!" declares the LORD. Therefore this is what the LORD, the God of Israel, says to the shepherds who tend my people: "Because you have scattered my flock and driven them away and have not bestowed care on them, I will bestow punishment on you for the evil you have done," declares the LORD. "I myself will gather the remnant of my flock out of all the countries where I have driven them and will bring them back to their pasture, where they will be fruitful and increase in number. I will place shepherds over them who will tend them, and they will no longer be afraid or terrified, nor will any be missing," declares the LORD.

"The days are coming," declares the LORD,

"when I will raise up for David a righteous Branch,

a King who will reign wisely
>   and do what is just and right in the land.
In his days Judah will be saved
>   and Israel will live in safety.
This is the name by which he will be called:
>   The LORD Our Righteous Savior.

"So then, the days are coming," declares the LORD, "when people will no longer say, 'As surely as the LORD lives, who brought the Israelites up out of Egypt,' but they will say, 'As surely as the LORD lives, who brought the descendants of Israel up out of the land of the north and out of all the countries where he had banished them.' Then they will live in their own land."

Concerning the prophets:
>   My heart is broken within me;
>>   all my bones tremble.
> I am like a drunken man,
>>   like a strong man overcome by wine,
> because of the LORD
>>   and his holy words.
> The land is full of adulterers;
>>   because of the curse the land lies parched
>>   and the pastures in the wilderness are withered.
> The prophets follow an evil course
>>   and use their power unjustly.

"Both prophet and priest are godless;
>   even in my temple I find their wickedness,"
>>   declares the LORD.
"Therefore their path will become slippery;
>   they will be banished to darkness
>   and there they will fall.
I will bring disaster on them
>   in the year they are punished,"
>>   declares the LORD.

"Among the prophets of Samaria
  I saw this repulsive thing:
They prophesied by Baal
  and led my people Israel astray.
And among the prophets of Jerusalem
  I have seen something horrible:
  They commit adultery and live a lie.
They strengthen the hands of evildoers,
  so that not one of them turns from their wickedness.
They are all like Sodom to me;
  the people of Jerusalem are like Gomorrah."
Therefore this is what the LORD Almighty says concerning the prophets:
  "I will make them eat bitter food
  and drink poisoned water,
because from the prophets of Jerusalem
  ungodliness has spread throughout the land."
This is what the LORD Almighty says:
  "Do not listen to what the prophets are prophesying to you;
  they fill you with false hopes.
They speak visions from their own minds,
  not from the mouth of the LORD.
They keep saying to those who despise me,
  'The LORD says: You will have peace.'
And to all who follow the stubbornness of their hearts
  they say, 'No harm will come to you.'"

What is one key insight that stands out to you from this passage?

_____

_____

_____

Consider as you listen to Mark's teaching, *why does the prophet Jeremiah warn about false teachers, and what does he prophesy about Jesus?*

Watch ▶

Play the video segment for session 8. As you watch, use the following outline to record any thoughts or concepts that stand out to you.

NOTES

——— The Problems People Have with Christianity ———

Christianity is viewed as:

- anti-homosexual
- judgmental
- hypocritical

> Modern people contend that the greatest proof God doesn't exist is the behavior of Christians themselves.
>
> —MARK CLARK

For some it's the Christian faith they reject; for others, it's religion in general.

> Good people will do good things; bad people will do bad things. But for good people to do bad things—that takes religion.
>
> —STEVEN WEINBERG

Some people believe the beliefs of religious people are dangerous.
A common challenge for skeptics: The historical and present-day religious violence.

-------- **How Do We, as Christians, Respond to These Claims?** --------

1. Admit some of the charges are true.

> Christians should not take the challenge of those injustices naïvely. We've got to approach them humbly, admitting that people have hurt other people in the name of Christianity. And we should apologize and repent of those actions.
>
> —MARK CLARK

Confession booth idea: Donald Miller, *Blue Like Jazz*.

> "The time has come," he said. "The kingdom of God has come near. Repent and believe the good news!"
>
> —MARK 1:15

Christians need to take responsibility for institutions that carry the name of Jesus.

2. Be aware of the fake disciples and hypocrisy within the church.

> "Watch out for false prophets. They come to you in sheep's clothing, but inwardly they are ferocious wolves."
>
> —MATTHEW 7:15

> "Not everyone who says to me, 'Lord, Lord,' will enter the kingdom of heaven, but only the one who does the will of my Father who is in heaven. Many will say to me on that day, 'Lord, Lord, did we not prophesy in your name and in your name drive out demons and in your name perform many miracles?' Then I will tell them plainly, 'I never knew you. Away from me, you evildoers!'"
>
> —MATTHEW 7:21–23

Christianity is not good advice to help good people lead moral lives. It's good news about Jesus, who he was, what he did.

> —MARK CLARK

We must judge Christianity based on Jesus and his teachings, not on people. Be wary of cultural Christianity.

"So, because you are lukewarm—neither hot nor cold—I am about to spit you out of my mouth."

—REVELATION 3:16

"Woe to you, teachers of the law and Pharisees, you hypocrites!"

—MATTHEW 23:13

Warning of hypocrisy: Matthew 23.

"Then I will tell them plainly, 'I never knew you. Away from me, you evildoers!'"

—MATTHEW 7:23

The fruit of the Spirit:

But the fruit of the Spirit is love, joy, peace, forbearance, kindness, goodness, faithfulness, gentleness and self-control. Against such things there is no law.

—GALATIANS 5:22–23

Example: Lifestyle activities of those who claim to be Christians vs. those who don't claim to be Christian at all.

• *gambling*	• *physical fighting or abuse*
• *online pornography*	• *illegal or nonprescription drugs*
• *stealing*	• *lying*
• *gossiping*	• *revenge*
• *consulting a medium or psychic*	• *drunkenness*

There was no statistical difference in these ten areas of a person's life between Christians and non-Christians.

Hypocritical Christians misrepresent Jesus to the world.

We must assess the Christian worldview based on the teaching of Jesus, not simply on the people who follow this worldview.

——— Jesus as the Essence of Christianity ———

What did Jesus teach?

> Attack me, rather than the path I follow, and which I point out to anyone who asks me where I think it lies. If I know the way home and am walking along it drunkenly, is it any less the right way because I am staggering from side to side?
>
> —LEO TOLSTOY

Following Jesus does not mean Christians are more moral than others.

> True Christians can't be separated from the evidence of the fruit of their lives.
>
> —MARK CLARK

> Even the demons believe that—and shudder.
>
> —JAMES 2:19

> You see that a person is considered righteous by what they do and not by faith alone.
>
> —JAMES 2:24

> As the body without the spirit is dead, so faith without deeds is dead.
>
> —JAMES 2:26

——— The Church as a Place for Sinners ———

Christianity is not about teaching people how to be good; it's about the good news of Jesus.

> Jesus lived a perfect life because we can't.
>
> —MARK CLARK

The church is a hospital: a gathering of broken, messed up people.

> Let your conversation be always full of grace, seasoned with salt, so that you may know how to answer everyone.
>
> —COLOSSIANS 4:6

Key Question: What are you judging Christianity on?
Key Question: Where did this church person start, where did they come from?

——— The Violent History of Christianity ———

Historical Revisionism: Exaggerations

One of the greatest tasks for the church today is to rescue Christianity from misunderstanding.
Alister McGrath
Facts vs. Mythology

> The world of facts is sometimes less interesting than myth, but it's necessary work.
>
> —MARK CLARK

The Crusades and Inquisition: *What happened?*
People refer to the Crusades as "religious wars."

> At the time of the Crusades and the Inquisition, Western Europe was fighting geopolitical wars while being culturally Christian.
>
> —MARK CLARK

Church and state were not separate at the time, so nationalistic battles looked like religious battles.
The Roman empire became Christian under Emperor Constantine in the 4th century.

> Rome continued to expand through conquest and violence. Christianity was absorbed and hijacked by the agenda of the Roman empire at that time. And Rome continued to do what it had always done: fighting battles to expand its worldly kingdom.
>
> —MARK CLARK

The Kingdom of God vs. the State

> Jesus said, "My kingdom is not of this world. If it were, my servants would fight to prevent my arrest by the Jewish leaders. But now my kingdom is from another place."
>
> —JOHN 18:36

> Take a modern example like Northern Ireland. It's often argued that the Protestants and the Catholics of Northern Ireland are fighting a religious war. They're not arguing about doctrine. They're not killing each other over transubstantiation, and baptism, or the doctrine of the justification by faith. Their fighting is for autonomy, retribution, and ultimately, who gets to run the country. The fight is not between committed followers of Jesus who want to ensure that people have pure doctrine and believe the truth. They are political freedom fighters.
>
> —TIMOTHY KELLER

We rarely see instances of the church waging war throughout history.

Violence is antithetical to the spirit of Christianity.

Jesus warns of the temptation of Christians to be in power over others:

> Then James and John, the sons of Zebedee, came to him. "Teacher," they said, "we want you to do for us whatever we ask."
>
> "What do you want me to do for you?" he asked.
>
> They replied, "Let one of us sit at your right and the other at your left in your glory."
>
> "You don't know what you are asking," Jesus said.
>
> —MARK 10:35–38

Christianity is about love, not power.

> But I tell you, love your enemies and pray for those who persecute you."
>
> —MATTHEW 5:44

Jesus never led a revolt.

Christianity has a self-correcting effort built into it.

Anything that hurts or marginalizes people in the name of Christ is a literal rejection of everything Jesus himself is about.

—MARK CLARK

The Witch Hunts

The church in Europe killed 5 million women during the witch trials over four centuries.

No one knows how many supposed witches the church killed altogether. Perhaps hundreds of thousands, perhaps millions.

—CARL SAGAN, *THE DEMON-HAUNTED WORLD*

Most scholars claim the accurate count is closer to 40,000–60,000 people killed in witch trials, 20% of whom were men.

The Salem Witch Trials: The reality is there were fewer than 25 people tried as witches, 19 of whom were sentenced to death and a few others who died in captivity.

The Accurate Sum of Violence

All of this violence adds up to the deaths of 200,000–250,000 people at the hands of "Christians" over the course of 500 years.

This is tragic, but not the numbers we see in modern mythology.

The Mythology of Religion as "Poison"

Religion poisons everything. The violence, the hatred in the world, it almost all arises from religion. Atheism will remove all the divisive reasons humankind kills and oppresses one another.

—CHRISTOPHER HITCHENS

But this argument doesn't make sense for the following reasons:

• Religious worldviews aren't the only systems of belief that result in violence.

The twentieth century gave rise to one of the greatest and most distressing paradoxes of human history, that the greatest intolerance and violence of that century were practiced by those who believed that religion causes intolerance and violence.

—ALISTER MCGRATH

When God is removed from society, he's simply replaced by other ideas that drive behavior.

Humankind is relentlessly religious. If we don't make one thing transcendent, we'll replace it with something else.

—MARK CLARK

• Modern atrocities are not Christian.

Any abortion clinic bombing, the responsibility is to all Christians. Each Christian must bear the responsibility and give account for it.

—DANIEL C. DENNETT

Key Question: Who bears the responsibility for atheistic atrocities?
Key Question: Which religion best avoids the injustices we all hate?
Atheism: Only the fittest survive.
Christianity: All people are made in the image of God.

So God created mankind in his own image,
    in the image of God he created them;
    male and female he created them.

—GENESIS 1:27

Slavery: It was Christianity that said slavery was wrong.
Example: William Wilberforce

——— Christianity Is for Hypocritical Humans ———

Christianity is not for perfect people, and Jesus went to the cross because of our sin. Through his resurrection, he saves us from our hypocrisy as humans.

> If you confess with your lips that Jesus is Lord and believe in your heart that God raised him from the dead, you will be saved.
>
> —ROMANS 10:9 RSV

> Christianity is not about the perfect lives of Christians, but the perfect life of Christ.
>
> —MARK CLARK

——— The Church Is for Sinners ———

Key Question: What should the church look like?

The church is going to be a messy place because it's full of sinners.

The church has often failed. But thanks be to God that our faith is not about the church but about Jesus.

Jesus is the only one worthy of our trust and imitation.

Group Discussion

Take a few minutes with your group members to discuss what you just watched and explore these concepts in Scripture. Then take time to pray together as a group. Use the space at the end of this session to keep track of prayer requests and group updates.

1. What stood out to you from Mark's teaching on the problem of hypocrisy?

_____

_____

_____

2. How have you experienced the hypocrisy of people or institutions who claim to be faith-based or specifically Christian?

_____

_____

_____

3. How do you respond to someone who is skeptical or who has been hurt by the hypocrisy of Christianity? How do you point them to the person of Jesus instead of the sin and violence of people who claim to be Christians as they commit injustices?

_____

_____

_____

4. **Read Matthew 7:15–20.** How do we know if a faith-filled person is reflecting Jesus or their own geopolitical or misguided spiritual perspectives? What does Jesus mean by "good fruit"?

_____

_____

_____

5. **Read Galatians 5.** What does the apostle Paul say it means to be called to freedom and walk by the Spirit? According to him, what is the "good fruit" of those who claim to be in Christ?

_____

_____

_____

6. **Read Mark 1:14–15.** One of the greatest commands Jesus gives the church, besides that of love, is the command to "repent and believe." How does repentance change our perspective? What kind of hypocrisy do we need to repent of as a Christian community? And if this is a safe space to do so, share one or two ways you need to individually repent of hypocrisy in your own life.

_____

_____

_____

Pray

Pray as a group before you close your time together. If you're struggling with the collective responsibility of Christian hypocrisy, pray about it. Ask God to give you a heart of understanding about the importance of collective and individual repentance for the hypocrisy we participate in as Christians. Thank God for salvation through Jesus, because we are sinners in need of a Savior, and for the good fruit he bears in our lives, often in spite of us. Use this space to keep track of prayer requests and group updates.

SESSION 8

Between-Sessions
PERSONAL STUDY

Weekly Reflection

Before you begin the between-sessions exercises, briefly review your video notes for session 8. In the space below, write down the *most significant point* you took away from this session.

_____

_____

_____

_____

Take some time to reflect on the material you covered during your group time by engaging in any or all of the following between-sessions exercises. As you read and experience the material, you may want to make a few notes in your guide. The primary goal of these between-sessions activities is for your own spiritual growth and personal reflection, and it is not a requirement for group participation. If you haven't done so already, read chapter eight in *The Problem of God*.

Day 1: The First Step of Fighting Hypocrisy
Read: *Matthew 11:20–30; Luke 3:1–22; Luke 13*

Consider: The way Christians behave is solid proof for a lot of modern people that what Christians believe is not true, and the greatest proof to the modern skeptic that God does not exist. The top reasons to not believe in Christianity cited by skeptics are because Christians are mean-spirited, judgmental, and have participated in historical violence at an alarming rate in the name of God, including the killing and torturing in the Crusades, the Inquisition, and the Witch Hunt trials. These realities and perceptions are enough to keep people from believing in Christ. While the perceptions of these realities are not always based on facts, some of these charges are absolutely true. And the first thing we must do as Christians is to admit the truth of some of these injustices.

Throughout history, many who call themselves Christians have done, and are doing, horrible things in the name of Christ. This is especially true when religion becomes a systematized, institutionalized, and politicized organization that wields political and military power over others—all of which we see Jesus was against. Christians should not take the challenge of admittance and repentance lightly when horrific acts have been committed in the name of Christ. We must approach them humbly, admitting that people have hurt other people in the name of Christianity. This is the first real step in fighting hypocrisy among Christians: to apologize for and repent for collective actions done under the banner of Christianity that have caused so much harm to others.

Reflect: Take a few moments to reflect on your answers to these questions.

How have you participated in the collective hypocrisy of Christianity?

_____

_____

_____

What does Jesus have to say about a refusal to repent in Matthew 11 and Luke 13? And what does he offer for those who are willing to repent and come to him?

_____

_____

_____

What can you do to take repentant actions for both your individual sins and for the collective sins of Christianity?

_____

_____

_____

Pray: Close out your time today by praying to ask God for forgiveness regarding the ways you've acted hypocritically. May your eyes be opened to the ways you've personally contributed to collective Christian hypocrisy.

Day 2: The Church and Hypocrisy
Read: *Matthew 23; Galatians 5:19–26; Ephesians 5*

Consider: There's a reason for the existence of hypocrisy in the church, both throughout history and in modern times. That's because the church is filled *with* people who are sinful, messy humans and *by* people who aren't actually Christians. This might be an obvious point for those of us who realize the church is for broken people and skeptics, meaning, the church is for *all of us*. But for the armchair critics who hold Christians responsible for every violent or unjust act done by any crazy person who claims to be a Christian or has a Jesus bumper sticker on their car, they need to realize the church is not made up of perfect people who all profess to be Christians. The church is made up of sinful people who are imperfect and in need of a perfect Savior to make things right with God.

We must also be aware that there are false teachers and false disciples embedded in the Christian church who lead people astray in false doctrine, false beliefs, false lives, and hypocritical behavior. This is why Jesus encourages people to focus on Jesus himself, and why he warns people not to judge Christianity by the morality of the people who try to follow him. Christianity is not simply good advice to help good people lead moral lives—that's cultural Christianity. But real Christianity is the good news about Jesus—who he was and what he did.

The point is, the atrocities done in the name of Christianity are often not done because the teachings of Christianity are bad, but because some people who claim to follow Christ don't actually know him or follow him. They may show up in church on Sundays, but they do not bear the "good fruit" of the life of Jesus—the Christian life. True Christians can't be separated from the evidence of the fruit in their lives. The church is meant to be the place where we work out our collective and individual mess and bear good fruit together as we follow the teachings of Jesus in community.

Reflect: Take a few moments to reflect on your answers to these questions.

How did Jesus respond to hypocrisy in his day? How does this message stand true for us today?

_____

_____

_____

Think about Galatians 5. Is it possible to act hypocritical and still reflect the fruits of the Spirit? How are the works of the flesh (NIV) incompatible with the fruits of the Spirit?

_____

_____

_____

How does Ephesians 5 describe the true disciples of Jesus?

_____

_____

_____

Pray: Close out your time today by praying to God about the hypocrisy found in the church through false teachers and false disciples. May God make the truth clear to you on what it means to be a disciple of Jesus.

Day 3: The Trivial Objection of Truth
Read: *Matthew 22:41–46; Mark 12:35–40; John 20*

Consider: When a person refuses to believe in God based on the actions of another person or a group throughout history, this is called a trivial objection. Scholars define a trivial objection as "focusing critical attention on a point less significant than the main point or basic thrust of an argument." And here's what I mean by trivial objection: Would anyone decide to throw out Einstein's mathematics because we found out he's a kleptomaniac—a thief? He wasn't, but there are people who would make that kind of objection upon uncovering such a belief. Einstein's mathematics would still stand true today even if he were accused of stealing from time to time. And to object would be a *trivial objection* of truth.

The same is true for Christianity. When hypocrisy and sinful actions are brought to bear on the question of whether or not Christianity is true, this is a misguided effort to object to the truth. It's using inconsequential data as a roadblock to finding the truth. Evaluating whether or not Christianity, or any other belief for that matter, is true must be based on research and data, not whether particular people adhere to its teachings. When we judge the entire Christian belief based on one broken human, then the "truth" hinges on the success or failure of sinful human beings, rather than the finished work of Jesus. We cannot put off the invitation of God and the truth of Christianity because of speculations about our next-door neighbors or what we've read in books. We must either accept or deny the invitation of God through the life and teachings of Jesus where there is no room for trivial objections of truth.

Reflect: Take a few moments to reflect on your answers to these questions.

What do these passages say about the truth of Jesus?

_____

_____

_____

Why do some accept his truth, while others reject it?

_____

_____

_____

Making people accept the truth of Jesus is not our responsibility. According to Matthew 22, what is our responsibility as we point others to the life and teachings of Jesus?

_____

_____

_____

Pray: Close out your time today by praying to God about the truth of God as reflected in the life of Jesus, whether or not it's always reflected in the lives of humanity.

For Next Week: Read chapter nine in *The Problem of God* and use the space below to write any insights or questions from your personal study that you want to discuss at the next group meeting.

Journal, Reflections, and Notes

The Problem of
EXCLUSIVITY

"I am the way and the truth and the life. No one comes to the Father except through me."

—JOHN 14:6

Welcome

The central claim that Jesus is the only way to God, in other words, the *exclusivity* of the Christian faith, is perhaps the most controversial claim in modern times. For many, this idea leaves a bad taste in our mouths. Even Christians wrestle with the notion of exclusivity, especially if we've traveled or consistently interact with people of other cultures and are regularly exposed to the religions of the wider world. I'll be honest, I still struggle with the exclusivity of Jesus every day, and I'm a pastor in a Christian church. I wrestle with it because day in and day out, I see beautiful people of different faiths and convictions.

Yet, if I believe the claims of Jesus to be true, I must acknowledge these people are wrong about God and need to be saved from their sin by Jesus and Jesus alone. This is an unsettling idea . . . until we lean into the logic and rationale of Christianity. When we do this, we will see that the Christian claim of exclusivity is the most honest position of all. And it has the power to shape our lives when we're willing to put our faith and trust fully in this belief. Is it offensive to some people to claim there is only one way to God? Yes. But do I still believe it? Yes. Let's dive in a little deeper together on this idea of Christian exclusivity.

Share 💬

To kick things off, briefly discuss one of the following:

- Name a time when you had to defend your Christian faith as the exclusive way to God.

  —*or*—

- What common questions do you hear or do you have about the exclusive claims of the Christian faith?

Read 📖

Invite someone to read aloud the following passage as preparation for Mark's teaching. Listen for fresh insights as you hear the verses being read, and then briefly discuss the questions that follow.

ISAIAH 42:1–16

"Here is my servant, whom I uphold,
>   my chosen one in whom I delight;
I will put my Spirit on him,
>   and he will bring justice to the nations.
He will not shout or cry out,
>   or raise his voice in the streets.
A bruised reed he will not break,
>   and a smoldering wick he will not snuff out.
In faithfulness he will bring forth justice;
>   he will not falter or be discouraged
till he establishes justice on earth.
>   In his teaching the islands will put their hope."

This is what God the LORD says—
the Creator of the heavens, who stretches them out,
>   who spreads out the earth with all that springs from it,
>   who gives breath to its people,
>   and life to those who walk on it:

"I, the LORD, have called you in righteousness;
　　I will take hold of your hand.
I will keep you and will make you
　　　to be a covenant for the people
　　　and a light for the Gentiles,
to open eyes that are blind,
　　　to free captives from prison
　　　and to release from the dungeon those who sit in darkness.

"I am the LORD; that is my name!
　　I will not yield my glory to another
　　or my praise to idols.
See, the former things have taken place,
　　and new things I declare;
before they spring into being
　　I announce them to you."

Sing to the LORD a new song,
　　his praise from the ends of the earth,
you who go down to the sea, and all that is in it,
　　you islands, and all who live in them.
Let the wilderness and its towns raise their voices;
　　let the settlements where Kedar lives rejoice.
Let the people of Sela sing for joy;
　　let them shout from the mountaintops.
Let them give glory to the LORD
　　and proclaim his praise in the islands.
The LORD will march out like a champion,
　　like a warrior he will stir up his zeal;
with a shout he will raise the battle cry
　　and will triumph over his enemies.

"For a long time I have kept silent,
     I have been quiet and held myself back.
But now, like a woman in childbirth,
     I cry out, I gasp and pant.
I will lay waste the mountains and hills
     and dry up all their vegetation;
I will turn rivers into islands
     and dry up the pools.
I will lead the blind by ways they have not known,
     along unfamiliar paths I will guide them;
I will turn the darkness into light before them
     and make the rough places smooth.
These are the things I will do;
     I will not forsake them."

What is one key insight that stands out to you from this passage?

_____

_____

_____

Consider as you listen to Mark's teaching, *how does the prophet Isaiah point to the exclusive way of Christ?*

_____

_____

_____

Watch ▶

Play the video segment for session 9. As you watch, use the following outline to record any thoughts or concepts that stand out to you.

NOTES

——— Our Existence ———

The only worldview worth living is one which answers the foundational questions of our existence. Christianity addresses each of those compellingly.

—MARK CLARK

THE FOUNDATIONAL QUESTIONS OF OUR EXISTENCE

Who are we?

What's the problem?

What's the solution?

A central claim of Christianity: *Jesus alone connects us to God and answers these questions about salvation, heaven, peace, and ultimate joy in life.*

——— The Problem of Exclusivity ———

Jesus is the only way or the exclusive means by which a person can connect to God and experience salvation in their life.

Critics claim this belief is narrow-minded and bigoted.

Most of us wrestle with the idea of exclusivity.

——— Inclusivism ———

Inclusivism is the idea that no one has a lock on the truth, that all religions have some measure of truth within them. There are different paths to God. All religions and worldviews are true.

Talladega Nights (movie).

The roots of inclusivism come from Eastern philosophy and are largely adopted in Western culture.

I am absolutely against any religion that says one faith is superior to another. I don't see how that is anything different than spiritual racism.

—RABBI SHMULEY BOTEACH

My position is that all great religions are fundamentally equal.

—GANDHI

I believe what Jesus and Mohammed and all the rest said was right.

—JOHN LENNON

One of the biggest mistakes humans make is to believe there's only one way. Actually, there are many diverse paths leading to God.

—OPRAH WINFREY

Believing in a single belief is seen as narrow-minded and judgmental.

——— Shalom ———

But Jesus claims one true religion.

Key Question: So how do we work to bring about shalom, or peace, with people who do not believe in one true God or religion?

Sometimes we fail because we do not see that at least for this issue and on this occasion, Muslims, Mormons, or Marxists might share the same goals and support the same plan as Christians.

—JOHN STACKHOUSE

The Parable of the Talents:

"His master replied, 'Well done, good and faithful servant! You have been faithful with a few things; I will put you in charge of many things. Come and share your master's happiness!'"

—MATTHEW 25:23

"His master replied, 'You wicked, lazy servant! So you knew that I harvest where I have not sown and gather where I have not scattered seed?'"

—MATTHEW 25:26

> The definition of faithfulness here is results. It is effectiveness and not just effort, even as some would prefer to view the story.
>
> —JOHN STACKHOUSE

Christianity involves working in the world toward certain goals in the service of Jesus.
Christian cooperation does not mean agreement in everything.
We mistake cultural pluralism with metaphysical pluralism.

Cultural Pluralism	Metaphysical Pluralism

> We can fight for people's rights to say what they believe. But we do not have to conclude that what they believe is true.
>
> —MARK CLARK

Christian civility does not commit us to a relativistic perspective. Civility doesn't require us to approve of what other people believe and do. It is one thing to insist that other people have the right to express their basic convictions. It is another thing to say that they are right in doing so.

> —RICHARD MOUW

Metaphysical pluralism is rooted more in emotional sentiment than reason or logic.

——— The Exclusivity of Other Religions ———

Islam: There is one God, Allah, and Muhammad is his prophet

Buddhism: There is one way to experience Nirvana

Hinduism: There are many ways that all contribute to the way one experiences Nirvana

Sikhism: There is one god and everyone is equal before god

Atheism: Rejects all beliefs beyond the material world altogether

> By trying to be inclusive, one by default actually becomes exclusivist.
>
> —MARK CLARK

——— The Truth of Christianity ———

> Jesus said to him, "I am the way, and the truth, and the life; no one comes to the Father, but by me."
>
> —JOHN 14:6 RSV

> "And there is salvation in no one else, for there is no other name under heaven given among men by which we must be saved."
>
> —ACTS 4:12 RSV

This is the cornerstone of Christianity.

People need to hear about Jesus in order to know about God.

Skeptics claim the Christian belief in Jesus is a Western worldview.

> Suppose we concede that if I had been born of Muslim parents rather than Christian parents, my beliefs would have been quite different. The same goes for the pluralist. If the pluralist had been born in Morocco, he probably wouldn't be a pluralist. Does it follow that his pluralist beliefs are produced in him by an unreliable process? Even though the pluralist views are a direct product of where he was born, he would deny that his beliefs are unreliable because of that factor. The same is true for the Christian.
>
> —ALVIN PLANTINGA

──────── **The Logical Impossibility of Inclusivism** ────────

The Principle of Noncontradiction: If something is true, its opposite can't be true at the same time in the same way.

All religions cannot be the same.

Most religions present *very different* teachings on the tenets of faith, and they contradict each other.

> We all agreed on the statement, that if Christians are right about Jesus being God, then Muslims and Jews fail in a serious way to love God as God really is. But if Muslims and Jews are right, Jesus is not God, but rather a teacher or a prophet, then Christians fail in a serious way to love God as God really is. The religious leaders recognized we couldn't all be right at the same time. Several of the students were quite disturbed by this because to insist that one faith has a better grasp on truth than others, was seen as intolerant.
>
> —TIMOTHY KELLER

Inclusivism excludes the exclusivists.

> It is more rational and respectful to say one religion is true than to say all religions are true.
>
> —MARK CLARK

All ideas are not equal, and all religions are not equally valid.

> The better route forward is to weigh facts and ideas against one another in order to find the view of life that is consistently true, makes sense of the world, produces measurable improvement in the lives of those who believe it and practice it, and lines up with truth in regards to history and philosophy and science and archaeology.
>
> —MARK CLARK

Different religions as different paths to the same place.
The analogy of the four blind men and the elephant:

The story is constantly told in order to neutralize the affirmation of the great religions, to suggest that they learn humility and recognize that none of them can have more than one aspect of the truth. But of course, the real point of the story is the exact opposite. The story is told by someone who can see and is the immensely arrogant claim of one who sees the full truth all the worlds' religions are only groping after. It embodies the claim to know the full reality which it claims that religions can't.

—LESSLIE NEWBIGIN

Key Question: What is the truth?

———— Mining for Truth ————

Settling for untruths in the name of getting along is negligent in every other sphere of life.

—MARK CLARK

The sacrifice of real answers to real questions.
Christianity as a "crutch for the weak."
The comfort of Christianity.
Defending Christianity.

"And you will know the truth, and the truth will make you free."

—JOHN 8:32 RSV

———— The Freedom of Christianity ————

Freedom and comfort are the fruit of believing the truth of Christianity.

If we abandon the search for truth, we will never really experience freedom.

—MARK CLARK

Group Discussion

Take a few minutes with your group members to discuss what you just watched and explore these concepts in Scripture. Then take time to pray together as a group. Use the space at the end of this session to keep track of prayer requests and group updates.

1. What stood out to you from Mark's teaching on the problem of exclusivity?

    _____

    _____

    _____

2. How would you summarize the way Mark explains human comfort and freedom in the exclusivity of Christ? Why is this a hard concept for so many modern-day people to grasp?

    _____

    _____

    _____

3. **Read the Parable of the Talents in Matthew 25:14–30, and verses 31–46.** What point is Jesus trying to make in the parable and the verses that follow, and how does it all relate to the exclusivity of Christ? According to the parable, what are the results of faithfulness in Jesus?

    _____

    _____

    _____

4. **Read John 8:31–47.** How does Jesus claim to be the only way to the Father? Why is this significant for his Jewish audience?

    _____

    _____

    _____

5. **Read John 14.** Why is it important for the disciples to understand the comfort of Christ in conjunction with the truth claims of Christ?

_____

_____

_____

6. How has this teaching cleared up the questions and confusion you have about the exclusive truth claims of the Christian faith? What other questions do you still have?

_____

_____

_____

Pray

Pray as a group before you close your time together. Thank God for the gift of salvation through Jesus. Ask God to continue to show you what it means to wholeheartedly believe in the truth of Jesus as the only way to God, and for the grace and strength to defend your faith when it's necessary to do so. Thank God for the love, comfort, and freedom he offers all of humanity through the sacrifice of Jesus. Use this space to keep track of prayer requests and group updates.

_____

_____

_____

_____

_____

_____

_____

_____

_____

_____

_____

Between-Sessions
PERSONAL STUDY

Weekly Reflection

Before you begin the between-sessions exercises, briefly review your video notes for session 9. In the space below, write down the *most significant point* you took away from this session.

_____

_____

_____

_____

Take some time to reflect on the material you covered during your group time by engaging in any or all of the following between-sessions exercises. As you read and experience the material, you may want to make a few notes in your guide. The primary goal of these between-sessions activities is for your own spiritual growth and personal reflection, and it is not a requirement for group participation. If you haven't done so already, read chapter nine in *The Problem of God*.

Day 1: The Cooperation of Christianity
Read: *Deuteronomy 6:1–19; Matthew 22:34–40; Mark 12:28–34; Matthew 28:16–20*

Consider: During my last year in college, I was informed I had missed a high school credit required for graduation and would have to go back to high school if I wanted to get my degree. After I got over the initial shock of this news, I signed up for summer school at a local high school. It was a memorable experience, to say the least. My teacher thought I was a genius. After writing a few essays and completing a few assignments, he called me to his desk and asked me what the deal was. The gig was up. It wasn't that I was a brilliant high school student; the fact was that I was almost done with college.

Occasionally, he and I would spar in class over philosophy in front of the rest of the students. He was very anti-Christian in his teaching. I would push back, trying to clear up any misrepresentations, mindful of my classmates who were listening. Outside of class, I spent time telling them about Jesus and teaching them how to improve their writing. I became friends with one of the Muslim girls in my class as we talked about our faith and compared worldviews and even argued about whose faith was more historically accurate. One day I showed up late for class but found out the teacher made fun of her faith in front of the whole class. She asked me how I had the energy to constantly defend my faith with him. Eventually, I talked to the teacher and told him what he did to her was a hurtful thing to do. Thankfully, he agreed and apologized to her at the beginning of the next class in front of all of the students.

I began to realize that it is possible to coexist with those with whom we disagree. We can even defend their right to believe what they believe. But that doesn't mean we let up on the Christian claim to truth: *that Jesus is the only way to God*. Christianity says Jesus is the *exclusive* means to salvation—the only way to heaven, peace, and ultimate joy in life. Cooperation with the faith of others does not mean agreement in everything. It means grace and love in everything.

Reflect: Take a few moments to reflect on your answers to these questions.

How do the Great Commandment and the Great Commission express the tension of cooperating with the beliefs of others while claiming the exclusive truth of Christianity?

_____

_____

_____

What makes the exclusive claim of Jesus as God unique compared to other religions?

_____

_____

_____

How are you sharing the good news of Jesus, the comfort of God's love, and the freedom of God's presence with your friends, family, colleagues, and community?

_____

_____

_____

Pray: Close out your time today by praying to God about the cooperative claim of Christianity. May you love others as you love God, and yet still claim the exclusive truth of the gospel.

Day 2: The Untruth of Inclusivism
Read: *John 8:31–47; John 14:6–7; Acts 4:1–12*

Consider: Many Westerners have adopted the religion of "Western Nicety." It's a civic religious belief where everyone's views are true and right as long as we avoid conflict. Sound familiar? The people who tend to be most vocal about this are the same people who are highly critical of Christianity, often calling it "narrow-minded judgmentalism." They're happy to argue that all worldviews should be accepted as true. But the reality is that this inclusive stance actually becomes exclusive at its core. And here's why: Trying to be inclusive ironically ends up excluding the exclusivist, and the premise that says, "I have a particular/true/right way of thinking that *all* religions are true" is actually an exclusive premise. Inclusivism pushes back against the claims of Jesus and the apostles by arguing that there is no one truth, that multiple religions are true at the same time even though they contradict each other.

And yet in doing so, inclusivism cuts off the branch on which it sits. Claiming there is no absolute truth is itself a truth statement. It's a contradicting system of thought and therefore needs to be abandoned. The nature of truth claims is that if something is true, the opposite is false. It seems to me that it's more rational and respectful to say *one religion is true* than to say *all* religions are true. Christians respond to the needs of the world with love and grace because they believe people need to hear about Jesus or they can't know God in this life or the next. This is the truth of the exclusive claims of Christ.

Reflect: Take a few moments to reflect on your answers to these questions.

What stands out to you about the way Jesus' Jewish audience responds to him in John 8? Why is it so hard for them to believe Jesus is who he says he is?

How does the exclusive claim of Jesus as the "only way" contribute to the growth of the early church? How might that growth be different if Jesus showed up and proclaimed to be one of many ways?

What does the exclusive claim of Christ mean for you? How will you push back and stand firm against the untrue claim of inclusivism?

Pray: Close out your time today by praying to God about the untrue claim of inclusivism and the truth of Jesus' exclusivity. May God make the exclusive way of Jesus clearer to you.

Day 3: The Comfort of Christianity
Read: *2 Corinthians 1:1–11; 2 Corinthians 7:1–7; Philippians 2:1–18*

Consider: Growing up, I used to think religious people used Christianity as a crutch for their own weakness or discomfort; that their belief in God was simply how they found comfort and got through during difficult times. But in my teenage mind, this didn't make God real. Looking back now that I've been a Christian for a number of years, I must say that I didn't come to believe in Christianity because it was comforting. I believed it because, from my perspective, it was historically, philosophically, and scientifically true. All of these disciplines concluded and confirmed the legitimacy of the Christian faith.

And while I do believe that Christianity is the most comforting, hopeful, and beautiful worldview in the marketplace of ideas regarding the great debate of life, the reality is Christianity is not all that comforting at times. Just look at the life of Christian martyrs throughout history. Even today, Christians have to defend what they believe in almost every sphere of life. And this is not always comfortable. Yet at end of life I see the comfort in their eyes and hear the peace in their voice when they tell me they're not scared to die because they know where they're going. In those moments, I realize the comfort of Christianity doesn't negate its truth.

Comfort is the fruit of believing in Jesus, the one who tells us that the truth will set us free. If we abandon the search for truth because we're too eager to settle for comfort, then we never get to experience the fruit of truth: our freedom. And that is the greatest tragedy of all. So if you believe in the truth of Jesus, and in the freedom of that decision, there you will find God's comfort.

Reflect: Take a few moments to reflect on your answers to these questions.

Notice how the apostle Paul talks about the relationship between suffering, distress, and comfort. How has the distress or suffering of someone else produced comfort for you, and vice versa?

_____

_____

_____

According to Paul's letter in 2 Corinthians 7, how does the comfort of one person lead to the comfort of others? How has this been true for you?

_____

_____

_____

According to Philippians 2, what commands are given to those who have found comfort in God's love?

_____

_____

_____

Pray: Close out your time today by praying to God about the comfort that comes as a result of believing in the truth of Christ. May you bear the fruit of God's loving comfort as you live in the freedom of Jesus.

For Next Week: Read chapter ten in *The Problem of God* and use the space below to write any insights or questions from your personal study that you want to discuss at the next group meeting.

Journal, Reflections, and Notes

The Problem of
JESUS

"I am the resurrection and the life."

—JOHN 11:25

Welcome

A lot of people *like* Jesus, even respect him as a teacher or a leader, and as a revolutionary, but they refuse to claim Jesus as God. They don't worship him or follow him with their lives because they aren't convinced that he really was God. And truthfully, I thought the same thing as a seventeen-year-old young man. At that stage in my life, I thought about little else but girls, partying, and the next drug I could try. Becoming a Christian wasn't really on my radar because I wasn't ready to give up my selfish ways of living. And when I finally found Jesus, I wasn't drawn to him for personal benefits. Instead, I was compelled by a conviction that the story of Jesus was true, and if it was, I had to abandon my life and plans for his.

In true God-like fashion, Jesus comes along and shatters the notion of what we think we have to do to earn our way to God: help old ladies across the street, avoid watching certain movies, pray so many times a day. At one point most of us thought God would be impressed with this kind of commitment to him and deem us worthy to be saved. But that's not what Jesus says. Jesus comes along and with his whole life, his ministry, and his message, he tells us that nothing we do to be saved will ever work. Nothing. The only way to salvation in God is *through Jesus*. On the cross, Jesus let evil do its worst, and then he rose again victorious. This isn't fan fiction, a myth, or a symbol. *It's reality*. And *that's* why I am a Christian today. I'm a Christian today because Jesus is God. I'm a Christian because the tomb is empty *for real*, and not just in a wishful thinking kind of way. But the tomb isn't empty just for me; it's empty for you, too. This is the problem of Jesus.

Share 💬

To kick things off, briefly discuss one of the following:

- Name one question you would ask Jesus if you could meet him in person today.
  —or—
- If you could interview one person from all of history, who would it be and why?

Read 📖

Invite someone to read aloud the following passage as preparation for Mark's teaching. Listen for fresh insights as you hear the verses being read, and then briefly discuss the questions that follow.

PSALM 118

> Give thanks to the LORD, for he is good;
>> his love endures forever.
>
> Let Israel say:
>> "His love endures forever."
> Let the house of Aaron say:
>> "His love endures forever."
> Let those who fear the LORD say:
>> "His love endures forever."
>
> When hard pressed, I cried to the LORD;
>> he brought me into a spacious place.
> The LORD is with me; I will not be afraid.
>> What can mere mortals do to me?
> The LORD is with me; he is my helper.
>> I look in triumph on my enemies.

It is better to take refuge in the LORD
>   than to trust in humans.
It is better to take refuge in the LORD
>   than to trust in princes.
All the nations surrounded me,
>   but in the name of the LORD I cut them down.
They surrounded me on every side,
>   but in the name of the LORD I cut them down.
They swarmed around me like bees,
>   but they were consumed as quickly as burning thorns;
>   in the name of the LORD I cut them down.
I was pushed back and about to fall,
>   but the LORD helped me.
The LORD is my strength and my defense;
>   he has become my salvation.

Shouts of joy and victory
>   resound in the tents of the righteous:
"The LORD's right hand has done mighty things!
>   The LORD's right hand is lifted high;
>   the LORD's right hand has done mighty things!"
I will not die but live,
>   and will proclaim what the LORD has done.
The LORD has chastened me severely,
>   but he has not given me over to death.
Open for me the gates of the righteous;
>   I will enter and give thanks to the LORD.
This is the gate of the LORD
>   through which the righteous may enter.
I will give you thanks, for you answered me;
>   you have become my salvation.

The stone the builders rejected
        has become the cornerstone;
the Lord has done this,
        and it is marvelous in our eyes.
The Lord has done it this very day;
        let us rejoice today and be glad.

Lord, save us!
        Lord, grant us success!

Blessed is he who comes in the name of the Lord.
        From the house of the Lord we bless you.
The Lord is God,
        and he has made his light shine on us.
With boughs in hand, join in the festal procession
        up to the horns of the altar.

You are my God, and I will praise you;
        you are my God, and I will exalt you.

Give thanks to the Lord, for he is good;
        his love endures forever.

What new insight do you notice in this passage regarding the coming of Jesus?

_____

_____

_____

Consider as you listen to Mark's teaching, *how does the love of God endure forever because of Jesus?*

_____

_____

_____

Watch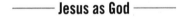

Play the video segment for session 10. As you watch, use the following outline to record any thoughts or concepts that stand out to you.

NOTES

——— **The Problem of Jesus** ———

The identity of Jesus is the central question of our lives.

—MARK CLARK

Key Questions

Did Jesus claim to be God?

If so, what did he ask people to do with that claim?

Where does that claim fit in relation to other religions in the marketplace of ideas?

——— **Jesus as God** ———

Jesus never said, "I am God."

The reality: Jesus' claims were understood in his historical-cultural context.

Jesus claimed to be God by using stories, questions, symbols, and activities recognized in the world in which he lived and taught.

> Among Pantheists, like Eastern Indian religions, anyone might say that he was part of God or one with God. There would be nothing very odd about it.
>
> —C. S. LEWIS

The Context of Jesus

- He's a Jewish teacher.
- He's part of a devout Jewish culture.
- People of his day believe in monotheism—one God.
- He identifies himself as Israel's God, not just any god.

The scandal is that among these Jews, there turns up a man who goes about talking as if he was God. And when you have grasped that, you will see that what this man said was quite simply the most shocking thing that has ever been uttered by human lips.

—C. S. LEWIS

"Now this is eternal life: that they know you, the only true God, and Jesus Christ, whom you have sent."

—JOHN 17:3

"God is not human, that he should lie, not a human being, that he should change his mind."

—NUMBERS 23:19

Jesus was charged with blasphemy for claiming he was God.

Again the high priest asked him, "Are you the Messiah, the Son of the Blessed One?" "I am," said Jesus. "And you will see the Son of Man sitting at the right hand of the Mighty One and coming on the clouds of heaven."

—MARK 14:61–62

"You have heard the blasphemy."

—MARK 14:64

Blasphemy: The act of claiming oneself the attributes and rights of God.

Jesus as God in Words and Deeds

Jesus' contemporaries, both those who became his followers and those who were determined not to become his followers, certainly regarded him as possessed of remarkable powers. The church did not invent the charge that Jesus was in league with Beelzebub [Satan]. But charges like that are not advanced unless they are needed as an explanation for some quite remarkable phenomenon.

—N. T. WRIGHT

The real difficulty, the supreme mystery with which the Gospel confronts us lies not in the Good Friday message of atonement nor in the Easter message of resurrection, but in the Christmas message of incarnation. This is the real stumbling block of Christianity.

—J. I. PACKER

Two reasons for the stumbling blocks:

1. People already have an idea of who God is and they can't fit Jesus into that.
2. People already have an idea of who Jesus is and they can't fit God into that.

Jesus challenges these stumbling blocks by:

1. He redefines his own identity.
2. He redefines God's identity.

What Others Believe about Jesus

Buddhism: Jesus was not God; he was an enlightened man like Buddha.

Hinduism: Jesus was one incarnation of God, similar to Krishna.

Islam: Jesus was a man, a prophet, a good leader, but is inferior to Muhammad.

Jehovah's Witnesses: Jesus was the archangel Michael—a created being who became a man.

Mormons: Jesus was only a man who became one of many gods; he was a polygamist and a half-brother of Lucifer.

New Age: Jesus is a state of consciousness we can all aspire to.

Scientology: Jesus was an implant forced upon Thetan a million years ago.

Key Question: Which one of these views of Jesus has any basis in history and facts?

Jesus' Claims to Be God

"Your father Abraham rejoiced that he was to see my day; he saw it and was glad." The Jews then said to him, "You are not yet fifty years old, and have you seen Abraham?" Jesus said to them, "Truly, truly, I say to you, before Abraham was, I am." So they took up stones to throw at him; but Jesus hid himself, and went out of the temple.

—JOHN 8:56–59 RSV

1. Jesus affirms that he existed as God before he was born in Bethlehem (Doctrine of Preexistence)—he claims he existed before Abraham.

> By this you know the Spirit of God: every spirit which confesses that Jesus Christ has come in the flesh is of God.
>
> —1 JOHN 4:2 RSV

> "And now, Father, glorify me in your presence with the glory I had with you before the world began."
>
> —JOHN 17:5

2. Jesus affirms he originated in heaven.

> "No one has ascended into heaven but he who descended from heaven, the Son of man."
>
> —JOHN 3:13 RSV

> "Truly, truly, I say to you, it was not Moses who gave you the bread from heaven; my Father gives you the true bread from heaven. For the bread of God is that which comes down from heaven, and gives life to the world." They said to him, "Lord, give us this bread always."
>
> —JOHN 6:32–34 RSV

3. Jesus claims to be not just God, but Israel's God.

> Jesus said to them, "Truly, truly, I say to you, before Abraham was, I am."
>
> —JOHN 8:58 RSV

> Then Moses said to God, "If I come to the people of Israel and say to them, 'The God of your fathers has sent me to you,' and they ask me, 'What is his name?' what shall I say to them?" God said to Moses, "I AM WHO I AM." And he said, "Say this to the people of Israel, 'I AM has sent me to you.'"
>
> —EXODUS 3:13–14 RSV

So they took up stones to throw at him; but Jesus hid himself, and went out of the temple.

—JOHN 8:59 RSV

In his defense Jesus said to them, "My Father is always at his work to this very day, and I too am working."

—JOHN 5:17

For this reason they tried all the more to kill him; not only was he breaking the Sabbath, but he was even calling God his own Father, making himself equal with God.

—JOHN 5:18

4. Jesus claims to participate in the Father's essential nature.

Jesus answered, "I did tell you, but you do not believe. The works I do in my Father's name testify about me, but you do not believe because you are not my sheep. My sheep listen to my voice; I know them, and they follow me. I give them eternal life, and they shall never perish; no one will snatch them out of my hand. My Father, who has given them to me, is greater than all; no one can snatch them out of my Father's hand. I and the Father are one."

—JOHN 10:25–30

The Trinity: There are three unique persons who make up the one God revealed to us in the Bible.

Jesus and God are one in essence and nature, but they are not one in the same person.

Again his Jewish opponents picked up stones to stone him, but Jesus said to them, "I have shown you many good works from the Father. For which of these do you stone me?" "We are not stoning you for any good work," they replied, "but for blasphemy, because you, a mere man, claim to be God."

—JOHN 10:31–33

Jesus never recants his claim to be God: Matthew 26; John 5; John 8; John 19.

Jesus' Teachings That Imply He Is God

1. Jesus taught people to pray to him (John 15; Acts 7; 1 Corinthians 1; Revelation 22).
2. Jesus accepted worship—something reserved for God (John 20:28).
3. Jesus said he was the only way to heaven (John 14).
4. Jesus came down from heaven (John 6).
5. Jesus claimed a number of titles used for God, such as Yahweh, Shepherd, I AM.

> Jesus claimed to be God through what he said, but he also demonstrated it by what he did.
>
> —MARK CLARK

Jesus Doing What Only God Can Do

1. Miracles
2. Fulfillment of who the Jews thought God was and what they thought God would do: *The temple, the healer, the new law, a new revelation of God.*

Early Christians Believed Jesus as God

1. His presence: *The temple*
2. His Torah: *The law*
3. The Word: *Wisdom*

> Early Christians had no intention of departing from Jewish-style monotheism, they would have insisted that they were searching out its true meaning.
>
> —N. T. WRIGHT

The early Christians were monotheistic, but they now saw Jesus as Israel's God.

> In the beginning was the Word, and the Word was with God, and the Word was God.
>
> —JOHN 1:1

The Word became flesh and made his dwelling among us.

—JOHN 1:14

Before me every knee will bow;

by me every tongue will swear.

—ISAIAH 45:23

In your relationships with one another, have the same mindset as Christ Jesus:

Who, being in very nature God,

did not consider equality with God something to be used to his own advantage;

rather, he made himself nothing

by taking the very nature of a servant,

being made in human likeness.

And being found in appearance as a man,

he humbled himself

by becoming obedient to death—

even death on a cross!

Therefore God exalted him to the highest place

and gave him the name that is above every name,

that at the name of Jesus every knee should bow,

in heaven and on earth and under the earth,

and every tongue acknowledge that Jesus Christ is Lord,

to the glory of God the Father.

—PHILIPPIANS 2:5–11

Jesus is Lord.

For in Christ all the fullness of the Deity lives in bodily form.

—COLOSSIANS 2:9

> Have this mind among yourselves, which is yours in Christ Jesus, who, though he was
> in the form of God, did not count equality with God a thing to be grasped.
> —PHILIPPIANS 2:5–6 RSV

Grasped means *to be held onto or kept.*

The Jews were the last people to believe God would take on a human form as was the case for Jesus.

> Thomas answered him, "My Lord and my God!"
> —JOHN 20:28 RSV

Key Question: Why did anyone actually believe Jesus?

The Resurrection of Jesus

The resurrection of Jesus showed that Jesus was who he claimed to be.
It led to the movement of the Christian church.

> If Christ has not been raised, your faith is futile and you are still in your sins. Then
> those also who have fallen asleep in Christ have perished. If for this life only we have
> hoped in Christ, we are of all men most to be pitied.
> —1 CORINTHIANS 15:17–19 RSV

If Jesus really rose from the dead, he must be followed.
Key Question: Should we believe Jesus' claim of the resurrection?
Reasons to believe it:

- The claims of the early church.
- Ancient historians and non-Christians who claimed Jesus was resurrected.
- The unexplainable phenomena of the quick and unique birth of the early church.
- The body of Jesus has never been found.

The Jews were claiming that their leader, Jesus of Nazareth, had risen from the dead and they were worshiping him as God.

—JOSEPHUS

Early Christians:

- Started meeting on Sundays to commemorate the resurrection of Jesus.
- They were persecuted by others.
- They died for the claim of the resurrection of Jesus.

Jesus claimed his own death and resurrection before it took place.

Key Question: Will we give ourselves and our lives to Jesus?

The risk and challenge of Christianity is a beautiful invitation made through the death and resurrection of Jesus.

Group Discussion

Take a few minutes with your group members to discuss what you just watched and explore these concepts in Scripture. Then take time to pray together as a group. Use the space at the end of this session to keep track of prayer requests and group updates.

1. What stood out to you from Mark's teaching on the problem of Jesus?

2. Why were Jesus' claims to be God *blasphemous* in ancient Jewish culture? Which claim would have been the hardest claim to accept for the early Jews, from your perspective?

3. **Read John 16:16–33.** Why was it so significant that Jesus talked about the resurrection before it actually took place? How did these conversations with Jesus and the actual resurrection change the way the disciples and followers of Jesus lived their lives?

4. **Read John 17.** Jesus not only claimed to be God, but his teachings also implied he was God. How does Jesus claim and imply that he's God in this passage?

5. **Read Philippians 2:1–18.** According to the apostle Paul, if we truly believe in the death and resurrection of Jesus, how are we to live our lives? What beliefs and actions show that we are "imitating Christ"?

6. Have you accepted the beautiful invitation of Jesus and given your life to God through him? If so, how has this changed you? If not, what are you waiting for, or what questions still need to be answered?

Pray

Pray as a group before you close your time together. Thank God for the gift of Jesus—for his life, his teachings, his claims to be God, his death, and his resurrection. If you are still struggling to accept Jesus as God, ask God to make the presence of Jesus known to you. May you know the power of Jesus' claims and experience the healing love of his teachings throughout Scripture. And may you trust Jesus with your heart and your life. Use this space to keep track of prayer requests and group updates.

Final
PERSONAL STUDY

Weekly Reflection

Before you begin the between-sessions exercises, briefly review your video notes for session 10. In the space below, write down the *most significant point* you took away from this session.

_____

_____

_____

_____

Take some time to reflect on the material you covered during your group time by engaging in any or all of the following exercises. As you read and experience the material, you may want to make a few notes in your guide. Because this is the last session, the primary goal of these activities is for your own spiritual growth and personal reflection. If you haven't done so already, read chapter ten in *The Problem of God*.

> **Day 1:** The Identity of Jesus
> **Read:** *Mark 14:53–64; Luke 24:13–27; John 6:25–59*

Consider: The identity of Jesus is the central question of our lives. It is the question around which all others orbit. I meet people all the time who say they like Jesus and respect him as a teacher and a revolutionary, but they don't worship him or follow him because they're not convinced of his identity, that he was God. In fact, there are still people wondering if Jesus actually claimed to be God because he never plainly said, "I am God." Fair enough. That's why we have to dig into the foundational questions about Jesus before we determine the implications for how we are to live. If Jesus is God, and he taught his followers that he is God, and it can be demonstrated that he is God in some way, then we should follow him and give our lives to him.

While we do not have a written record of Jesus putting those exact words together to claim, "I am God," in the New Testament, he had many other ways to do it, and he made the most of those ways every chance he had, in every way that *mattered*. Jesus claimed clearly and directly to be God in a way that was clear to his own culture and is still clear to us today. To make this claim, Jesus utilized stories, symbols, and activities that were recognized in the world in which he taught. And if we miss this, then we miss the identity of Jesus because he never used the exact words we are looking for in the precise sequential order we are expecting. That's why it's crucial for us to first see Jesus in his historical-cultural context, rather than our own, to understand what he claims about himself. If we don't, we will likely misunderstand or twist what he was saying.

Reflect: Take a few moments to reflect on your answers to these questions.

In what ways does Jesus make the connection between himself and the God of the Old Testament?

_____

_____

_____

How does Jesus describe himself in these passages?

_____

_____

_____

What makes you put your faith and trust in Jesus and his claim to be God?

_____

_____

_____

Pray: Close out your time today by praying to God about the identity of Jesus. May you see, hear, and understand the claims of the identity of Jesus.

Day 2: Jesus as the Incarnational Presence of God
Read: *Mark 11:15–19; Matthew 4:19; 8:22; 9:9; Psalm 14:7; John 17*

Consider: In first-century Judaism, God was not a created being, but there were symbols that pointed to God's incarnational presence in the world. *Incarnation* simply means "into meat" or "in the flesh." So when people talked of God, who is an immaterial spirit, becoming human and taking on flesh and blood, it was called "incarnation." But there were other incarnational ways God showed up before Jesus—in the temple, the Torah, and the understanding that God had promised to return to Jerusalem one day. And then Jesus shows up and claims to be God incarnate by also claiming to be the fulfillment of each and every one of the formative symbols within Jewish life. He also claims to bring the end and final fulfillment of all that these symbols meant and were ever meant to mean.

It's needless to say, this caused quite a stir. The temple was where God's presence resided *and* where people's sins were forgiven through sacrifices. Jesus claimed to be the fulfillment of the temple, acting as if the temple was no longer necessary because of his presence. The Torah was the Old Testament Law. Jesus claimed to be the fulfillment of the Torah—the very reason it existed. Salvation was no longer possible through obedience to the Torah, but through Jesus as the new Torah. Loyalty to God and his law took on a new form in loyalty to Jesus. The Torah also spoke about the promise of God's long-awaited return to Jerusalem, which would bring both judgment and salvation to Israel and the whole world. Jesus claimed to be the fulfillment of God's promised return to Jerusalem. He claimed to be the final judgment and salvation for the world. Jesus specifically lives, speaks, and acts in ways that reveal the incarnational presence of God through him.

Reflect: Take a few moments to reflect on your answers to these questions.

How does the passage in Mark point to the fulfillment of Jesus as the temple?

_____

_____

_____

Why was Jesus' command to "follow me" so subversive for first-century Jews who were following the law of the Torah?

_____

_____

_____

What does Jesus' prayer at the beginning of John 17 reveal to his disciples? How does this reveal Jesus as the salvation for Israel that comes out of Zion (Psalm 14:7)?

_____

_____

_____

Pray: Close out your time today by praying to God about his incarnational presence in Jesus. May you believe in Jesus as the fulfillment of God's promises.

Day 3: The Disruption of Truth
Read: *Psalm 101; Proverbs 30:7–9; 1 John 4*

Consider: Let's be honest. For many of us, if we're comfortable and our needs are being met, we're hesitant to question the problem of God and the claims of Jesus too deeply because it might mean changing things—and we aren't sure we'll like it. The prospect of a different reality due to our conviction in Jesus frightens us and feels like anything *but* freedom. In other words, some of us would rather *not* be saved than be faced with the unknown of what salvation means for us. We'd rather live the lie of the status quo than the uncertainty of truth. *The truth sets us free only if we want it to.*

This reminds me of the time my grandfather was "abducted" by a young couple. My brother and I went to visit my grandfather only to discover he was no longer living in the apartment he owned for over fifty years. He was now living in a big, brand-new home with complete strangers. We were suspicious of the situation, knowing it was a popular scam among couples in Vancouver who couldn't afford homes in expensive neighborhoods on their own. So the scammers would find and befriend an elderly, lonely, often near-death person, convince that person to come to live with them, and in the process sink all of that person's money into a big, beautiful new home where they all live together. By the time we found my grandfather and explained the situation, he simply smiled back at us and said he didn't want to leave. He didn't want to know the truth if he was indeed being scammed because he was comfortable and not as lonely in his new luxury. Even if his situation was based on a lie, it seemed to him like a worthy trade.

I think this is a picture of the way many people think about the things we've explored throughout this book. If God is real and if the claims of Jesus are real, then that's a problem because it upends life as we know it. This is the disruption of the truth of Jesus.

Reflect: Take a few moments to reflect on your answers to these questions.

How do these first two passages warn us about lies and encourage us to practice the truth?

_____

_____

_____

Testing the truth is important to the apostle John. According to him, how do we test the spirits and recognize the Spirit of God?

_____

_____

_____

The greatest good of accepting the disruptive and truthful claims of Jesus as Christ is the love of God. How has the love of God changed your life?

_____

_____

_____

Pray: Close out your time today by praying to God about the disruptive truth of Jesus. May you be willing to choose the uncertainty of truth over the comfort of false claims and lies.

Journal, Reflections, and Notes

_____

_____

_____

_____

_____

_____

_____

_____

_____

Closing Words

Thank you for joining me for *The Problem of God*. It has been a joy to walk alongside each one of you on your quest for clarity regarding God. This study was inspired by the questions raised by many of you, the very same questions I still wrestle with as a person and as a pastor on a daily basis.

As I researched and wrote *The Problem of God*, I was inspired by the apostle Paul who went to the strategic areas of his time—Athens, Corinth, Ephesus, and Rome—and spoke into the marketplace of ideas. He explained how the gospel and the biblical story interfaced with those ideas, interacted with the thinkers and philosophers of the time, and showed how Jesus is the one true God and the center of all things (Acts 17–20). Now, I realize that I'm not the apostle Paul and that the arguments I've presented may not fully convince you to become a follower of Jesus. But it is my prayer that in the journey, you have seen that Christianity offers a compelling, alternative, and *true* vision of the world.

But I'd be remiss if I didn't remind you that the problem of God requires a decision. If God is real, if the claims of Jesus are true, if there really is a heaven and hell, if Jesus is the exclusive way to know God—then that's a problem in need of a decision. God upsets our comfortable lives where we have the illusion of being in control and offers us an opportunity to change and be transformed.

So, will you trust the one who came to save us, the one who will lead us to the true harbor, however shaky the boat ride might seem right now? This is the problematic invitation of God, made possible by the hope of Jesus Christ. And such has been the point of this journey.

It is my hope and prayer that, as a result of this invitation, you're willing to open yourself up to God's vision for your life—for all of our lives. May you be willing to listen and go where the evidence leads, to question your questions, and doubt your doubts. May you be willing to believe in things that scare you, and follow God to places you never dreamed of—the places God wants to lead you rather than the places you've agreed to go on your own terms.

Peace to you,

MARK CLARK

Index of Verses
USED (BY SESSION)

Session 1	Session 2	Session 3	Session 4
Opening Verse Genesis 1:1	**Opening Verse** Ecclesiastes 3:11	**Opening Verse** Jeremiah 31:33	**Opening Verse** Colossians 2:17
Read Psalm 104	**Read** Psalm 145	**Read** Psalm 119:1–35	**Read** Isaiah 53
Video Romans 1:20 RSV	**Video** Romans 2:15 RSV John 4:24 RSV	**Video** Romans 1:20 Mark 16:9–20	**Video** Romans 2:15–16 RSV Colossians 2:17 RSV
Group Discussion Colossians 1:15–17 Ecclesiastes 1:1–18	**Group Discussion** Romans 2:12–16 Job 11:7–9	John 7:53–8:11 Jeremiah 31:31, 33 ESV Colossians 3:22 Colossians 3 John 5 Luke 24:32	**Group Discussion** Luke 7:24–30 Matthew 11:7–15 Colossians 2
Personal Study John 1:14 John 8:31–47 1 Thessalonians 5:19–22 Genesis 1 Psalm 8 Psalm 104 Acts 14:16–18 John 4:11–21 Romans 1:18–23 1 John 4:11–21	**Personal Study** Romans 2:12–16 James 1 Colossians 1:15–20 Hebrews 11:1–3 Revelation 4:11 Jeremiah 10:11–13 John 1:1–5 John 4:23–24 2 Peter 3:1–9	**Group Discussion** 2 Timothy 3:16–17 Jeremiah 31:31–34 **Personal Study** Luke 24:13–27 Hebrews 11 Mark 16:9–20 John 7:53–8:11 2 Timothy 3:14–17 Colossians 2:6–17 Acts 10 Galatians 3:10–14	**Personal Study** Matthew 2 Daniel 5 1 Timothy 1:1–7 1 Timothy 4 2 Timothy 4:1–8 Romans 2:12–16 Colossians 2:16–17 1 Corinthians 15:3–49

Session 5	Session 6	Session 7	Session 8
Opening Verse Romans 8:28	**Opening Verse** Luke 13:28	**Opening Verse** James 1:17	**Opening Verse** Luke 6:43 ESV
Read Ecclesiastes 3	**Read** Luke 16:19–31	**Read** Proverbs 5	**Read** Jeremiah 23:1–17
Video Genesis 3 Revelation 6:9–10 RSV Ecclesiastes 3:11 Genesis 1–2 Romans 8:28 Romans 8:18 ESV	**Video** Matthew 25:41, 46 RSV Matthew 8:12 Mark 9:43, 48 ESV Matthew 11: 21–24 RSV John 5 Matthew 25 Revelation 20 Romans 2 Matthew 7 Mark 9 Hebrews 12:29 Luke 16 Matthew 25	**Video** Genesis 1:25 Genesis 1:31 1 Corinthians 7:1–3 1 Corinthians 7:5 1 Corinthians 7:4 Ephesians 5:33 Proverbs 5:18–19 Song of Songs 7:7–8 Song of Songs 5:1 Matthew 22:30 James 1:17	**Video** Mark 1:15 Matthew 7:15 Matthew 7:21–23 Revelation 3:16 Matthew 23:13 Matthew 7:23 Galatians 5:22–23 James 2:19 James 2:24 James 2:26 Colossians 4:6 John 18:36 Mark 10:35–38 Matthew 5:44 Genesis 1:27 Romans 10:9 RSV
Group Discussion Genesis 22:1–14 Romans 8:18–39	**Group Discussion** Matthew 25:31–46 Mark 9:42–50	**Group Discussion** Song of Songs 7 1 Corinthians 7:1–16 and 25–40 Ephesians 5:25–33	**Group Discussion** Matthew 7:15–20 Galatians 5 Mark 1:14–15
Personal Study Psalm 6 Habakkuk 1–3 Job 1–2 and 40–42 John 3:1–21 John 5:16–23 Philippians 2:1–11	**Personal Study** Proverbs 9:1–12 Philippians 2:12–18 Matthew 7:13–20 Matthew 8:5–13 Mark 9:42–49 Matthew 13:24–43 Luke 13:22–28 Revelation 20	**Personal Study** Genesis 1:25–31 Deuteronomy 24:5 Proverbs 5:15–21 1 Corinthians 7:1–7 Song of Songs 1–7 Matthew 22:30 Ephesians 5 1 Corinthians 6:13–20 James 1:1–18	**Personal Study** Matthew 11:20–30 Luke 3:1–22 Luke 13 Matthew 23 Galatians 5:19–26 Ephesians 5 Matthew 22:41–46 Mark 12:35–40 John 20

Session 9	Session 10	
Opening Verse John 14:6	**Opening Verse** John 11:25	John 20:28 John 14 John 6
Read Isaiah 42:1–16	**Read** Psalm 118	John 1:1 John 1:14 Isaiah 45:23
Video Matthew 25:23 Matthew 25:26 John 14:6 RSV Acts 4:12 RSV John 8:32 RSV	**Video** John 17:3 Numbers 23:19 Mark 14:61–62 Mark 14:64 John 8:56–59 RSV 1 John 4:2 RSV	Philippians 2:5–11 Colossians 2:9 Philippians 2:5–6 RSV John 20:28 RSV 1 Corinthians 15:17–19 RSV
Group Discussion Matthew 25:14–46 John 8:31–47 John 14	John 17:5 John 3:13 RSV John 6:32–34 RSV John 8:58 RSV Exodus 3:13–14 RSV	**Group Discussion** John 16:16–33 John 17 Philippians 2:1–18
Personal Study Deuteronomy 6:1–19 Matthew 22:34–40 Mark 12:28–34 Matthew 28:16–20 John 8:31–47 John 14:6–7 Acts 4:1–12 2 Corinthians 1:1–11 2 Corinthians 7:1–7 Philippians 2:1–18	John 8:59 RSV John 5:17 John 5:18 John 10:25–30 John 10:31–33 Matthew 26 John 5, 8, 19 John 15 Acts 7 1 Corinthians 1 Revelation 22	**Personal Study** Mark 14:53–64 Luke 24:13–27 John 6:25–59 Mark 11:15–19 Matthew 4:19 8:22, 9:9 Psalm 14:7 John 17 Psalm 101 Proverbs 30:7–9 1 John 4

Leading This Group

Group Size

The Problem of God video study is designed to be experienced in a group setting such as a Bible study, Sunday school class, or any small group gathering. To ensure everyone has enough time to participate in discussions, it is recommended that large groups break up into smaller groups of four to six people each.

Materials Needed

Each participant should have his or her own study guide, which includes notes for video segments, directions for activities, and discussion questions, as well as personal studies to deepen learning between sessions.

Timing

Each session will take between two and three hours. For those who have less time available to meet, you can use fewer questions for discussion. You may also opt to devote two meetings to each session, covering one of the two parts of each session per meeting.

Facilitation

Each group should appoint a facilitator who is responsible for starting the video and for keeping track of time during discussions and activities. Facilitators may also read questions aloud and monitor discussions, prompting participants to respond and assuring that everyone has the opportunity to participate.

Personal Studies

Maximize the impact of the curriculum with additional study between group sessions. There are three days of personal study available for each session. Feel free to engage with these optional study materials as much or as little as you need.